Fluent in 3 Months

How Anyone at Any Age Can Learn to Speak Any Language from Anywhere in the World

Benny Lewis

HarperOne

An Imprint of HarperCollinsPublishers

HarperOne

HarperCollins books may be purchased for educational, business, or sales promotional use. For information, please e-mail the Special Markets Department at SPsales@harpercollins.com.

HarperCollins website: http://www.harpercollins.com

HarperCollins®, ®, and HarperOne™ are trademarks of HarperCollins Publishers.

FIRST EDITION

Designed by Terry McGrath

Library of Congress Cataloging-in-Publication Data
Lewis, Benny (Brendan Richard)
Fluent in 3 months : how anyone at any age can learn to speak any language from anywhere in the world / Benny Lewis. — First Edition.
    pages cm
ISBN 978-0-06-228269-9
1. Language and languages—Study and teaching. 2. Language and languages—Self-instruction. I. Title. II. Title: Fluent in three months.
P53.77.L49 2014
418.0071—dc23
                              2013034559

14 15 16 17 18 RRD(C) 10 9 8 7 6 5 4 3

Contents

ACKNOWLEDGMENTS

I would like, first and foremost, to thank all the many thousands of people who have showed me, over the span of a decade, how to have more faith in all people, from all countries, to appreciate communication, and to not worry about a few mistakes. I have almost never been judged as a beginning language learner, and it's thanks to these wonderful people of countless nationalities that I have been able to discover so many different cultures and make lifelong friends. Their patience has been infinite, and I am glad to say that they will be as kind to any reader of this book—any new language learner—as they were with me.

Also, a huge thank-you to Jorge, the first polyglot I met in my life, who is from Brazil and whose name I couldn't even pronounce when I met him. He inspired me to get started (bumpy as the start was) on this wonderful road to language learning.

While writing the book, the biggest help by far was my "polyNot" friend Anthony Lauder, who read through the entire first unedited draft and sent me feedback longer than the longest chapter of the book, which helped me realize the many ways I could improve my arguments. He also helped me appreciate the perspective of a newbie, who may find certain aspects of language learning difficult, though he himself has great skills and thoughts about language learning and has inspired many others to give it a try too.

Lauren Cutlip, M.A. in rhetoric, also helped me vastly improve arguments from the perspective of someone completely new to language learning, as well as present certain thoughts more clearly while maintaining my voice.

John Fotheringham from languagemastery.com helped me improve the Japanese section, since I was learning that language while in the editing stages of the book and needed someone with experience to present the language in an encouraging light. At press time, I've added Japanese to my list of languages.

Next is the group I lovingly call Team Linguist, all of whom have master's or Ph.D. degrees in various fields of linguistics. I sent them parts of the book to get their professional or academic opinions on the scientific validity of what I was saying. Their feedback was essential during fact-checking and ensured the book had a solid foundation beyond my experiences and anecdotes. Team Linguist included Agnieszka Mizuu Gorońska (M.A. in ethnolinguistics), Rachel Selby (M.A. in TESOL/language acquisition), Sarah McMonagle (Ph.D. in language policy and planning), Seonaid Beckwith (M.A. in psycholinguistics of second-language acquisition), and Judith Meyer (M.A. in computational linguistics; also a polyglot with her own site: Learnlangs.com).

My Story, Your Passion

> *Your story, like mine, begins and ends with passion—the surest path to learning a new language.*

In late July 2003, just a couple of weeks after my twenty-first birthday, I moved to Valencia, Spain. To help me adjust to life in a foreign country, I enrolled in a Spanish class.

It was a small class, and it was taught entirely in Spanish, which was a bit of a problem for me because I only understood English. I had just graduated with a degree in electronic engineering, and I had barely passed the German and Irish* courses I took in high school. Languages were definitely not my thing.

After several classes, I was getting absolutely nowhere. Each lesson ended with the other students wearing great big satisfied smiles on their faces. I knew they had figured out something

---

* Irish, or Gaeilge, is the standard name for the Celtic language of Ireland (not to be confused with Gaelic, the language of Scotland); our dialect of English is actually referred to as Hiberno English, or "Irish English," never "Irish."

about the language that they didn't know before, while I still couldn't understand a single word. My ego was destroyed. I was, without a doubt, the worst student in the class, and as I walked home with my head hung low, I couldn't help thinking, *It's not fair! Why were those guys blessed with the language learning gene and I wasn't? I'm never going to learn Spanish.*

After six months in Spain, I could barely muster up the courage to ask how much something cost or where the bathroom was. I really started to think I would never learn Spanish. I began to worry my experience immersed in a different country would be a total failure. I was convinced my destiny was to spend the rest of my life speaking only English.

Fast-forward seven years. One night in Budapest, I ended up at a "couchsurfing" party at a local bar with an international crowd. I confidently strolled in and said hello to everyone *in Hungarian,* one of the most notoriously difficult languages in the world. I started chatting with a local, *in Hungarian,* about my progress with his native language. I had been learning it only for about five weeks, but I was still able to have this rudimentary chat with him.

Next, I noticed a slight Brazilian Portuguese accent from the guy speaking English to my left. I asked, "Você é brasileiro?" (Are you Brazilian?), and when he told me, in Portuguese, that he was from Rio, I immediately switched to my Carioca accent, using slang from his own city, telling him how much I missed it. He was shocked to hear an Irish guy speak his own Portuguese dialect in a random bar in Budapest!

Then I recognized a Spanish friend of mine across the table and immediately switched to fluent Spanish, asking her how *her*

Hungarian was coming along. Later, a couple from Quebec arrived, and I turned on my Quebec accent and expressions while speaking French. We exchanged contact information and made plans to hang out the next day.

That night I also managed to use some Italian and Esperanto and wowed a Thai tourist with a few phrases of basic Thai, using all the right tones. I even flirted in German with a German girl I saw regularly at these meetings.

In one evening I spoke eight languages (including a little English) casually, socially, and naturally. I switched between them effortlessly, without mixing them up, and—more important—made some amazing new friends in the process.

Since then I've learned several other languages, and at the time of writing this, I can confidently use twelve languages in varying degrees of proficiency, from conversational (in Dutch, Mandarin Chinese, and American Sign Language) to certified mastery (in Spanish) and everything in between for the other nine. I understand the basics of another twelve languages on top of these. I also run Fluentin3months.com, the world's largest language learning blog, which, to date, has helped millions of people around the world learn a new language.

All of this is true despite the fact that I spoke only English until the age of twenty-one and did poorly in my attempts to learn languages in school.

How did this happen? How did I go from dropping out of my Spanish language class to being able to converse in more than a dozen languages? Simply by changing how I approach new languages.

The Way to Learn a Language Is to Live It

One of the biggest issues with a traditional approach to language learning is that the benefits to picking up a new language are constantly postponed. Study this and study that and *then*, if you're lucky, in a few years' time, you'll eventually understand the language. As well as being far from the truth, this approach removes the fun and the *life* from the process.

In many education systems, especially in English-speaking countries, languages are taught the same way as any other subject, like geography or history. Teachers provide the "facts" (vocabulary) so the student will "know" the language. Or, as in mathematics, students do the exercises to understand the "rules" (grammar).

Except on rare occasions, this approach does not produce *speakers* of the target language, so something clearly needs to be fixed. A language is a means of communication and should be *lived* rather than taught.

A teacher's primary role should be as a language facilitator. A teacher should make sure students use the target language at whatever level they happen to be at, rather than keep them quiet while he or she does all the talking, trying to transfer the informational components of the language into the students' brains.

In high school, I had to learn Irish. It was mandatory and, in order to gain admission to university, I needed to pass my exams. As a result, I only cared about learning enough Irish to pass; I didn't care about the language itself.

My attitude toward Irish changed completely when I actually took the time to live in the Gaeltacht region of Ireland, where people still speak the language, and I started to make friends using it.

The second language I took in high school was German. I took German because Germany is an important economy in Europe, and I figured it would look good to have this language on my résumé. German language skills would help me stand out, especially since most people in my year were studying French. Once again, I didn't care about the German language; I just thought learning it might give me secondary benefits. And, of course, I barely retained anything. I thought German was nothing more than *der, die, das* tables of impossible-to-learn grammar. And I imagined Germans were robots that automatically spit out grammatically correct sentences.

That is, until I met actual Germans and saw firsthand how interesting and fun they were. So fun, in fact, I wanted to get to know them better. This way of thinking allowed me to stop thinking of the German language as a barrier between Germans and me, but instead as a bridge I could cross to communicate with them. In both cases, my initial tangential motivations for learning a language were replaced by a direct motivation to live that language and use it as a means of communication and connection.

This is how language courses should work. The best tend to veer away from the traditional approach of drilling grammar and word lists into us, or providing us with old, boring, and irrelevant texts. Instead, the best courses encourage us to play games and role-play in the language. They let students speak the language with one another, which—as I realized with both of the languages I had learned poorly in high school and then much better as an adult—is the truest means of communication. As a result of speaking the language right away, students start to *acquire* the language rather than *learn* it as they would other academic subjects.

What's Your Motivation?

Let me ask you something: When you first tried to take on a language you were interested in, did you think something like, *If I learn this language then I'll get this benefit*—some benefit that had nothing to do with intrinsically communicating in that language or getting to know a foreign country's culture or people?

"Benefits," like career advancement, impressing people, prestige, passing an exam, crossing something off your bucket list, or other similar reasons, are examples of tangential motivations that have nothing to do with using the language itself.

For so many language learners, that motivation to learn a language is more often than not extrinsic rather than intrinsic. They have no true passion for the language; their only motivation is almost entirely for the side benefits they'd theoretically get from speaking a new language. Recognizing the bridges to *people* that language learning opens up as opposed to benefits you may receive someday, is a key ingredient to making language learning faster, more fun, and more efficient.

The Missing Ingredient: Passion

In this book, I focus on independent learners, rather than those sitting in classrooms. Even if you are taking a classroom course, whether it is taught efficiently or not, you need to be an efficient learner in your free time. When you love learning a language enough to have it fill your free time, then your passion can truly blossom. You can find many new motivations beyond extrinsic ones.

This is not to say that these factors automatically lead to failure; success in your career, for instance, can be a very effective motivating factor. The catch, however, is that these side benefits can't be the main motivators for you to learn a language if you want to learn the language better. You must intrinsically want to speak that language for the language or culture itself.

When I eventually rebooted my attempts to learn Spanish, I put aside these superficial reasons—that someday Spanish might make me impressive or perhaps even more employable. Instead, I started to learn Spanish specifically to use Spanish with other human beings. This made all the difference. I genuinely wanted to communicate in Spanish and make friends through their native tongue. I also wanted to get to know Spain beyond the superficial experience I had had until then.

I was no longer motivated by benefits I might get months or years in the future, or by the idea that speaking Spanish would "make me cool"; I was genuinely passionate about learning the language in order to communicate directly with and understand other people through reading, watching, and listening to Spanish.

So take a moment to ask yourself, what is your motivation for learning a new language? Are you learning a language for the "wrong" reasons? Even if you indeed need the benefits that result from learning a language, like advancing your career, can you mentally put aside the long-term benefits and embrace learning the language for the inherent beauty of it and the many doors it will open for you? If you change your thinking in this way, all the side benefits will come, but they will come much faster, because your new focus will make learning a language happen more quickly and efficiently.

The missing ingredient, and the single thing I have found that separates successful language learners from unsuccessful ones, is a passion for the language itself. For successful language learners, acquiring a new language is the reward.

Give Yourself Goose Bumps

So how do you develop this passion if extrinsic benefits have been clouding your vision?

For a start, seek out movies and art and history from the country where your target language is spoken, listen to music in that language, read books and magazines, find as many sources of audio, video, and text online as you can, and absolutely spend time with native speakers—which you'll notice I've dedicated an entire chapter to, without requiring that you travel to their countries.

Even when I know I am going to a country and have my flight booked, or even when I'm in the country itself, I can get lazy and make very slow progress *unless* I make that language a true part of my life. Doing so lets me grow passionate for the language.

Here's a good time to tell you about my friend Khatzumoto. After speaking and reading Japanese exclusively for just eighteen months, he could read technical materials and conduct business correspondence and job interviews, all in Japanese. He ultimately landed a job in Japan as a software engineer at a gigantic corporation based in Tokyo.

The amazing thing is that Khatzumoto reached this stage by living his life in Japanese . . . while in Utah! He filled his world with Japanese *virtually*. He watched anime, read manga, consumed his favorite sci-fi series dubbed in Japanese, and surrounded himself with everything Japanese during every spare moment of his day, even though he was a full-time computer science student. By integrating his target language into his day-to-day living, he gave himself no escape route; he had no choice but to live most of his days in Japanese. As a result, his passion for the language grew. Today, his motto for learning Japanese, or for learning any language, remains "You don't know a language, you live it. You don't learn a language, you get used to it."

Nothing creates passion for a language more than using it. Similarly, nothing I say about why you should learn a new language will be more convincing than the first time you understand your first sentence, or the first time you make yourself understood, in a different language. These moments will give you goose bumps, and the immense feeling of satisfaction that comes with them will stay with you forever, as well as thousands of other positive experiences that will follow.

The passion ingredient is what makes learning languages worthwhile; you simply have to live that language in whatever way you can to have your passion sparked. Spend time with natives of the language, listen to streamed radio, watch TV shows and movies, or read books in the language, and you will spark your passion, which will motivate much more progress than any side benefit could ever hope to inspire.

How Far Are You Willing to Go?

Moses McCormick is a well-known polyglot who often posts online videos in languages that he's learning. He can communicate, in varying degrees—from knowing a few phrases to being able to converse very well—in about fifty languages. When he was trying to improve his Hmong, an Asian language rarely known to Westerners, he told me the one place where he could consistently practice with native speakers was in online chat rooms. That's all well and good, but one major obstacle, he said, was that most chat rooms were often filled with men interested only in meeting girls. They weren't interested in continuing a conversation with another guy.

So what did Moses do? He created another screen name and logged in as a woman (a virtual sex change operation, if you will, only taking just an instant and totally reversible). Even when he said he was married, he still found that people were much more eager to chat.

Would you go to such lengths to get some practice time in your target language? If not, then maybe you aren't passionate enough to get the results!

I'm obviously not saying that logging into a chat room as another gender is a prerequisite for speaking another language, but going to such lengths and being willing to do whatever it takes, no matter what the level of embarrassment, will greatly improve your chances of being successful.

The Right Mentality Will Launch You Forward

Success in language learning doesn't come from having the perfect circumstances or require a perfect language learning system. Success relies heavily on facing challenges with the right mentality, having motivation and passion, and sticking to the learning process until you charge through the "brick wall" in your way.

Someone with mountains of passion will always find a way to progress in his or her target language, even if that person uses inefficient learning approaches or gets stuck on plateaus for long periods of time. There are successful language learners who learn very differently from me—sometimes slower, sometimes faster, sometimes with better language skills or more languages under their belts. Without fail, however, the one thing we always have in common is passion.

In fact, every language learning challenge I have ever taken on has had its disappointing failures. I've had moments when I felt like giving up, when I saw others doing much better than I was, and when I had trouble finding people to practice with. I've struggled with conversations that went nowhere, had some rough starts, hit plateaus, forgotten words I should have known, and experienced countless other obstacles that made me feel like a failure, all of which led to many hours of frustration. But I kept going because I *wanted* to keep going. I had a passion for language, and that's how I've been able to learn to speak twelve languages and counting.

Once you learn one new language, you're off and running. Learning the first foreign language gives you the skills to learn a second, and then a third, faster and more efficiently.

In the following pages, I'll show you how to master a new language, with the lessons I've learned and the techniques I've applied while transitioning from a monoglot to a polyglot, plus give you solutions to—or ways around—difficult problems. Believe me, none of it involves re-engineering your DNA to add in the language gene. Instead, this collection of lessons can be used by any language learner, at any stage or any age, and it includes the same lessons millions of people have already been using on my blog: Fluentin3months.com.

Follow Up

千里之行，始于足下

Qiānlǐ zhī xíng, shǐ yú zú xià.

"A journey of a thousand miles begins with a single step."

—CHINESE PROVERB

The first step in language learning is to make the commitment to do whatever it takes to make your project a success. If you have the passion to do what it takes, no matter what that may require, then this will ensure that you will, soon, be able to speak your target language.

For more on my story and other thoughts on the importance of passion in language learning, check out fi3m.com/intro, where there are videos, links to sites of people mentioned in this chapter, and extra updates designed specifically for readers of this introduction.

CHAPTER 1

Destroying Twenty Common Language Learning Myths

Stop making excuses. There's simply no reason you "can't" learn a new language, and I'll tell you why.

I can confidently say that any person on earth can learn a second language, no matter what their age, intelligence, working or living situation is, or what their past attempts to learn languages have been like. When our mentality, motivation, passion, and attitude are kept strong, we have the momentum required to charge on toward language fluency.

But there's a catch. Even with the best intentions and most enthusiastic starts, we are all bound to run into challenges along the way—sometimes before we even begin or at the very first step of the journey—that prevent us from really starting to learn the language.

The thing is, while these obstacles may feel like brick walls preventing us from continuing on our path toward speaking a language, many of them are actually myths that exist nowhere but in our minds.

The reasons we give for why we can't learn a language often have us second-guessing ourselves, wondering if all this language learning business isn't for us at all. Many may feel too old, untalented, busy, or located too far from any native speakers. There are a host of reasons, excuses, and discouragements we tell ourselves, have been told by others, or just presume to be true. Well, there is no good excuse for not learning a language and advancing toward fluency.

I have personally talked to thousands of language learners, with millions more reading my blog over the years, and I have heard about pretty much every possible setback learners have had (and I've had quite a few myself). In this chapter, I share with you the twenty most common retorts people have given me when I tell them they can, and should, learn a second language—some of these you have probably felt yourself—and I'll explain why each one of them is baseless, or at least has a good solution, as well as many examples of people who have overcome this challenge before.

1. Aren't Adult Language Learners at a Disadvantage?

One of the most common reasons many people give for not even trying to learn a language is that, once someone passes a certain age, learning a new language is pointless. This almost feels like common sense. "Children are better language learners," people often tell me, "and after a certain age you simply can't learn a language."

I know I certainly felt too old already, even at the age of twenty-one. However, the idea has never held any water or been demonstrated as true by any serious scientific study. Instead there is only a general trend of adults not learning languages as well as children—but this may be true for reasons totally unrelated to age. Adults struggle with new languages most especially because of a misguided learning approach, their learning environment, or their lack of enthusiasm for the task, all of which can be changed.

Fluency in a second language is definitely possible for all ages. The "I'm too old" excuse is one of many self-fulfilling prophecies we'll be coming across in this chapter. By telling yourself you are too old, you decide to not put in the work and, thus, don't learn the language. The vicious cycle continues.

The idea that babies have an advantage over us because their brains are hardwired to learn languages while ours aren't is also not the case. No matter what language you are taking on, you have a vast head start on any baby learning that language, simply because you cannot start from scratch as an adult learner! Starting from scratch is what is truly impossible. There is a huge difference between learning your first language and learning your second. Without the thousands of words that your second language may have in common with your first, a baby has to do much more work, work that we adult learners so merrily take for granted.

It took you years to be able to confidently distinguish between all the sounds in your native language. When you start to learn a new language as an adult, there are so many learning processes you get to skip that babies have to spend years working on. How about not needing to learn how to distinguish between sounds like an *m* and an *n*? Or all the other sounds that the majority of languages have in common? You also don't have to concern yourself with developing the muscles in your voice box and tongue in order to even *attempt* to make noises with them. Or with training your ear to be able to distinguish between male and female voices, or between the particular voices of family members and friends, not just other noises in your environment.

Adult language learners also have the advantage of already having been exposed to years of context in universal human interaction, which indicates when someone is angry, shouting, or asking a question, or the many other aspects of international body language, intonation, and speech volume. One study at the University of California, Los Angeles, actually found that an incredible 93 percent of communication of emotions is nonverbal. And a majority of nonverbal communication is universal. A laugh is a laugh, across the world.

While it's possible that some of these communication cues are built into our DNA to be recognized automatically, babies still need to develop them. They have all this extra work ahead of them, learning how to communicate in general terms before they can even begin to incorporate specific language blocks like vocabulary and grammar.

But a language is not just vocabulary and grammar; it's an entire spectrum of communication, from the clothes we wear to our posture, hand gestures, personal space, pauses, volume, intonation, and a host of other verbal and nonverbal cues, most of which are universal among modern cultures. (There are definitely exceptions, but if you compare them to the number of similarities, the latter will greatly outnumber the former.)

An infant picks all of this up over many years before he or she can adequately communicate with adults and other children. This means we adults have much more time and energy to focus on the much smaller aspects of communication, of how words go together. Babies have it hard, and young children still need serious tweaking, even at the age of six or so. This is why it takes years before children can be considered good speakers. But this shouldn't be the case for us. When it comes to language learning, an adult can overtake a baby any day because an adult has much less work to do.

Even if you're with me so far, you may still say that adults are definitely worse off than preteens and early teenagers, who already speak one language well. You might think that their brains are "fresher" or process new information more quickly than ours. Why bother competing with that?

This sounds logical enough, but research has shown that it's not true. A study by the University of Haifa in Israel examined how well different age groups—eight-year-olds, twelve-year-olds, and adults—picked up unexplained grammar rules. The study revealed that the "adults were consistently better in everything we measured."*

Adults are not *worse* language learners, but *different* language learners. The real problem with adult language learners is the environment in which we try to learn languages. As mentioned in the introduction, a traditional academic environment is already not efficient for children, but this is even more true for adults. If an adult makes a mistake, other adults are less likely to correct that person because they don't want to insult him or her, but the teacher–student dynamic with children makes this less of a problem.

A child learning a new language after a certain age can also find it quite hard if the material is presented too academically. In their spare time, children are more likely to want to play video games or enjoy activities not related to language learning. We can send them to an immersion school, where they can at least play games with other students in the right language, but they may not want to be there and are often just going because their parents have sent them. Their own rebellious nature may get the better of them and, even in an immersion environment, if they don't want to learn, they won't.

Adults, on the other hand, can actively decide to learn a language and justify doing so with many more reasons than a child may come up with, including a greater degree of passion. They can go out of their way to arrange to meet up with people

---

* Catherine de Lange, "Age No Excuse for Failing to Learn a New Language," *New Scientist*, July 22, 2011, 2822, http://www.newscientist.com/article/mg21128224.000-age-no-excuse-for-failing-to-learn-a-new-language.html#.UkRfbxBv58E.

to practice the language. Adults have many more options for language learning strategies, and can control their free time more easily than children can. Being the master of your own destiny has its perks! Resourceful and clever adults can even pick up a helpful book on the topic or read blog posts written by a charming Irish polyglot, for instance.

Adults are also more analytical than children. This creates different sets of advantages for both. Children will indeed be more likely to "pick up" a language with less conscious effort, but this does not mean they are better at it. Adults who put in a conscious effort can keep up at the same rate of progress, even if making that effort is a little more exhausting.

While I prefer to leave grammar aside (more on that later) until I can converse pretty well in a language, when I do get to it, I process the rules and understand the logic behind them much better than a child ever would. Children are better at absorbing a language naturally, but adults do that *and* combine it with a greater capacity to reason why one sentence works one way over another way.

Because of all this—plus implementing a human-centered learning approach—I feel I am a much better language learner now, in my thirties, than I ever was as an eight-, twelve-, sixteen-, or even twenty-year-old. I am getting better at learning languages with age, not worse!

What about when you get much older? I have come across people in their fifties, sixties, seventies, and even older starting with their first foreign language and succeeding. I regularly receive e-mails and comments on my blog from learners of these ages who are making fantastic progress in their target languages.

Ultimately, I don't want to argue that adults are *better* language learners than children, because this has the danger of discouraging those who want their children to do better. My point is that we all have our advantages, and it is much more practical to look at what those advantages are than to dwell on and exaggerate any challenges either group has.

It's never too late for an adult of any age to learn a new language.

The true advantage children have over adults is that they are naturally less afraid to make mistakes. Rather than feel this is a stamp for life, we should learn from children. Try to enjoy the language learning process and don't be afraid of a little embarrassment. Laugh at your mistakes and have fun with it, instead of being way too grown up about it or taking every minor slipup so seriously. In this sense, we can definitely learn from children!

Children tend to absorb their first few thousand words entirely by human interaction, whereas adults, learning another language, may learn these from textbooks. Learning exactly like a baby is not wise, but we can aim to emulate many of the aspects of a child's learning environment that encourage real communication.

Also, keep in mind that babies and young children effectively have full-time teachers—their parents—who laugh at their mistakes (thinking they are *cute*), have almost infinite patience, and are overjoyed at every success. Imagine if an adult could find a native speaker so motivated to help! These are things you can seek to emulate in your own environment, such as spending more time with native speakers motivated to help you. These are not inherent advantages built into children, but aspects of their environments from which you can draw inspiration.

2. I Don't Have the Language Gene

Lack of talent! Oh, if only I had a penny for every time I heard *this*! Here's a self-fulfilling prophecy if ever there was one.

When I was in school, I repeated to myself, *I don't have the language gene*. Since I didn't have it, I didn't put in the work to really learn German; and since I didn't put in the work, I barely passed my exams and ultimately didn't speak German after five years of lessons in the language. Therefore, I didn't have the language gene.

Do you see a problem with my circular logic here?

There is absolutely no reason to believe in a "language gene," as if the ability to learn a foreign language is encoded in your genome at conception. The truth is that if a multilingual gene really exists, we must all be born with it. Most of the planet actually speaks *more* than one language. Many places in the West have a huge number of inhabitants who speak two languages, like Quebec, Catalonia, and Switzerland, to name just three. In China, people switch between distinct varieties of

Chinese such as Mandarin and Cantonese with ease, and it's quite common in India to come across someone who can converse in five different languages.

In Luxembourg, the language of instruction changes every few years. As a result, children come out of school fluent in French, German, and Luxembourgish. If any of us had been brought up in that environment, we would have learned the same languages just as well, regardless of our genetics.

If you happen to be an American, don't forget that your heritage comes from countries that have plenty of people speaking multiple languages, or that one of your ancestors crossed the ocean perhaps speaking a different language than yours. *Somewhere* in your family tree someone very likely communicated in more than one language. Pulling the genetics card when this is the case in your own family tree is quite silly.

The fact that a monolingual culture breeds monolinguals doesn't say anything about an individual's inherent potential. When it comes to language learning, there is no room for doubt: you decide your own success. Do the necessary work to learn a language, and you'll catch up with—and even overtake—the "naturally talented."

3. I Don't Have the Time

It's all well and good for those with no full-time job or responsibilities to go gallivanting around the world and spend all day studying languages, but some of us have to *work*.

Definitely a fair retort, if it were true that successful language learners were only those who practice language learning full-time. But this is very far from what actually happens. If anything, those doing it full-time are a rarity, and pretty much all successful language learners I have met have done it while also working a full-time job, completing their undergraduate studies, helping to raise a family, taking care of loved ones, or juggling a host of other responsibilities.

For instance, the second foreign language I seriously took the time to learn was Italian. And though I did move to Italy while I was learning the language (though you really don't have to, as I'll discuss later), the job I took in Rome required me to work more than sixty hours a week, so I know better than most what it's like to have a *really* demanding schedule and still find a way to make language learning work.

It's not a question of having enough time. I've seen more cases than I care to list of people who had all day, every day, for many months to learn a language but squandered that time. It's all about *making* time. Even though I only had every other evening free in Rome, I used that tiny amount of time to focus on improving my skills in Italian. And while working as a receptionist at an international youth hostel, I often studied during the odd quiet moment when nobody was around.

Progress happens if you set aside the time to allow it to happen. Way too many of us waste endless hours watching TV, browsing Facebook and YouTube, shopping, drinking alcohol, and countless other activities. Think about all the moments throughout your day when time gets away from you. All those moments when you're simply waiting: waiting for an elevator, waiting in a shopping line, waiting for a friend to arrive, waiting for a bus or subway or any other type of public transportation. I always try to squeeze as much as I can out of these free moments. I whip out my smartphone and go through a few flash cards, or take a phrase book out of my pocket and review some essential basics. Or, if I'm feeling social and adventurous in a different country, I'll turn to the person behind me and try to strike up a quick conversation.

All of these little moments add up. They're hours of potential language learning or practice time. When you are dedicated to a language, there is not a single moment to waste.

For example, when I was learning Arabic, I activated an app on my phone that allowed me to use my camera to blend the view ahead of me into a flash-card app, so I could see where I was going while both studying *and* walking. (Of course, for most people, using audio studying tools while either walking or driving is more advisable.)

Make the time and change your priorities. Don't spread yourself thin. Focus on one major project and you will definitely have the time to do what it takes. Sure, being able to devote several months full-time to your project would be nice, but if that isn't possible, just devote as much time as you can and you will still reach the level you want to reach, even if the time it takes is longer.

Ultimately, it's not about the number of months or years, but the number of minutes every day you devote to this challenge. These minutes are what truly count.

4. Language Programs Are Expensive

Another huge misconception, especially in America, is that language learning is a privilege reserved for the rich. You have to pour money into expensive language learning courses, software, immersion programs, flights around the world, books, and private teachers—or you will fail miserably.

Not quite. I blame products like Rosetta Stone, which can cost several hundreds of dollars. I have tried Rosetta Stone myself, but I can't say it's superior to cheaper alternatives or free sources of information like online tools, blogs, or time with foreign friends. Spending more does not guarantee you'll succeed any more easily than someone who works with a much tighter budget. In fact, in a survey I ran on my blog, I found that spending money on several different products actually reduces your chances of success. You're far more likely to succeed if you pick just one basic product—like a phrase book, for instance—and set yourself to start speaking the language right away. Spending money, or hoarding language products, does nothing for your progress.

5. I'm Waiting for the Perfect Language Course

You can spend weeks or months saving up for a language learning course, but a course won't solve all your problems. In fact, it won't even solve most of them. Courses provide the content of a particular language but offer nothing concerning what you can actually do with that content.

To get started, I generally just grab a phrase book. This doesn't necessarily mean it's the best way for you, but my point is that even if a perfect course exists, it will still be only as good as the effort you put into using the language regularly.

After flipping through my phrase book, I go to my local bookstore and buy a course for between ten and twenty dollars, or visit a library to check one out for free. I generally find the Teach Yourself, Assimil, and Colloquial courses to be pretty good ones to start with, but there are also plenty of free online alternatives.

Does this mean that these are the perfect courses? No, but they are certainly quite good. They give me the general words and phrases I tend to use at the start in everyday conversations, while also missing others, such as vocabulary more specific to my situation—like that I studied engineering or that I write on a blog.

No course will ever be perfect. With that in mind, go get an affordable book or sign up for a free online course, like on Duolingo.com, and remember to do lots of language work on the side—activities that will keep you in genuine interactions with human beings.

That's why, instead of study material or a particular immersion course, I prefer to focus on whom I spend time with and how, conversing as often as possible in their language. A self-guided learning approach based on more structured study sessions works wonders.

6. The Wrong Learning Method Will Doom Me Before I Start

A lot of us feel that if we get off on the wrong foot, our early mistakes will sabotage an entire project. Nothing could be further from the truth. It's okay to have a bumpy start. The trick is to begin!

Even if you pick the wrong course, or you've tried one before and it didn't work out, that doesn't determine how things will go *this* time. And if you run into new challenges, pick yourself up, dust yourself off, and try again. A little persistence pays off.

Any energy you put into researching the best possible way to begin would always be better spent on actually learning and using the language.

7. I Need to Study Before I Can Have a Conversation

You should start to speak a new language from day one. This may seem counterintuitive. Many of us feel we need to study first, until that glorious day when we are "ready" and have "enough" words to finally have a real conversation.

The truth is that day will never come. You can always justify, even when you have all but mastered a language, that you are not ready. There will always be more words to learn, more grammar to perfect, and more work to tweak your accent. You just have to accept that there will be a few communication problems and you will deal with them.

This requires embracing a little imperfection, especially during the early stages. Use the language, even though you may slip up a little. Being okay with this is the trick to using the language now, rather than waiting many years.

8. I Can't Focus

My friend Scott Young wrote the exams for an entire MIT computer Science undergraduate program in one year, has a formal education in business, and studied psychology, nutrition, mathematics, physics, and economics. He is also a successful entrepreneur and enjoys life to the fullest. On top of this, he learned French in a short time, and the first time we met we spoke only in this language (even though he's from the English-speaking part of Canada). He has more recently had his very own projects to learn a language in three months, very similar to mine.

He clearly has quite a lot on his plate!

When I asked him about how on earth he keeps focused with all of these things going on, he told me that it's very simple: *focus on one major project at a time*. He stays committed to the priority project no matter what, even if distractions may tempt him to try to take on two or more interesting projects simultaneously.

Those with focus will make the various interests they have in life work sequentially rather than in parallel, so that they are not spreading themselves too thin. This way nothing gets neglected.

Focus is not an unusual trick, but it is a seldom-applied one. Scott gets so many things done by not attempting an overwhelming balancing act of divided interests. Instead, his method involves working patiently and systematically, adding each new skill to his life one at a time.

9. Some Languages Are Just Too Hard

It doesn't matter what language they're trying to learn—some people will always claim it's the hardest language in the world. I've heard it for every single language I've ever taken on, except Esperanto.

There is no "hardest" language. It's all biased opinions from proud natives who have no idea what it's like to learn that language as a second language, or from other learners who have learned it slowly and may feel their egos challenged if you try to learn it more quickly than they did. Discouragement is always for their benefit, not yours, and frankly, they have no idea what they are talking about.

When I publicly announced on my blog that I was going to learn Chinese, a lot of Westerners who had learned Chinese tried to discourage me (though never in person, and never did a native speaker do so). They went out of their way to repeat over and over again that all my previous experience was irrelevant because I was now learning the "hardest language in the world."

What I found, though, was that most of them had almost exclusively learned only Chinese. They had little to no experience with other languages. Many of them said European languages like French and Spanish were very easy, even though many learners and native speakers with much more experience in these languages disagreed. Also, it turned out Chinese wasn't that bad after all, and I explain why in detail in chapter 6.

Nobody wins in this comparison game. If you aren't learning other languages, then forget them and focus on the one you're truly passionate about. Think about the many reasons you want to learn a language, and dismiss outright any unhelpful discouragement about its difficulty.

A good attitude will get you far, no matter what language you're learning.

10. Plateaus Are Inevitable

Plateaus themselves are not myths. The fact that we have to be stuck on them is.

You won't run into this problem as a beginner, but you may a little further down the road. Some of us have no problem getting into a new language, and we successfully reach a certain point of either basic communication or conversational fluency. But then we get stuck.

Why is that? If we successfully reached this stage, surely we found the perfect method for us, right?

Not quite. The point is not to search endlessly for the "perfect" method, but to find a good one and adjust it as you go. You reach a plateau because something in your current approach is not allowing you to progress.

If what you're doing isn't working, it isn't good enough and needs to be changed. One of my favorite definitions of insanity is doing the same thing over and over again and expecting different results. So don't be afraid to mix things up. A change in how you think about a new language—or how often you speak it and with whom—will go a long way toward helping you avoid plateaus. Even if your previous approach did you well and got you to a particular stage, maybe a slightly new approach should be tried to catapult you to the next level.

11. Perfect Mastery Is Impossible

When people think that speaking a language means nothing less than being able to debate Kantian philosophy, with no accent or hesitations, then it can indeed feel like it would take decades to be able to say that you can actually speak a language. If you have this in mind, the entire project can feel hopeless. Why even bother starting if such an end goal is so impossible?

I don't know about you, but my English isn't perfect. I hesitate when I'm nervous, I forget precisely the right word every now and again, and there are plenty of topics I am uncomfortable talking about. Applying higher standards to your target language than you would to your native language is overkill.

Rest assured that fluency is very much possible for us mere mortals, even for those of us who did poorly in languages in school. Aim for a conversational level (or lower) first and then strive for fluency. Mastery can indeed come with time (even if perfection in *any* language is not possible), but have short-term goals first.

12. Languages Are Boring

A huge misconception in language learning is that it's all about studying the entire time.

If what you're doing is boring, then stop what you're doing. This doesn't mean that learning a language is boring, just that the way you're trying to do it right now is. There are so many interesting ways to progress in your language that don't require doing something dull.

Try to expose yourself to some alternative content in the language—like through its music, cartoons, movies, magazines, jokes, many of which are available online—find a different language exchange partner, or follow any approach that tickles your fancy. There are infinite possibilities for learning a new language. With all these options available to you, staying bored is ridiculous. Do something different and you won't be bored as easily.

13. Native Speakers Won't Speak to Me

When I was first learning Spanish, I was really afraid that I would accidentally call someone's mother a smelly grasshopper (or worse) if I slipped up my pronunciation or conjugations. Because of this, I felt I had to wait until my Spanish was much better before I dared to use it in front of other people.

The problem with this is that you never feel ready enough. There will always be more to learn, so you will always be able to make an excuse that you should go off and learn more words before trying to speak to people. It's a vicious cycle that keeps many of us from opening our mouths for years.

And what actually happens when you do? People are incredibly encouraging, helpful, so happy to hear you try, patient, and understanding. This idea that we'll frustrate native speakers is not based on experience (or if it is, we are greatly exaggerating or misinterpreting what happened); it's based on the *assumption* they'll make fun of us or lose patience. This is our own fear manifesting itself; it's not based on reality.

At some point in your life I am sure someone learning English tried to speak to you. Did their pronunciation and their awkward, halting use of words insult you? Did you laugh out loud and call them a fool for trying? Or did you instead listen patiently and try to understand and communicate with them, and think that it's great that they speak more than one language? This last scenario is what will certainly happen when you try too. I guarantee, in almost every situation, you will be glad you tried to speak a language.

As for native speakers who simply reply back to us in English, it happens to the best of us. There are simple ways around this issue, though, which I discuss in detail in chapter 5. A bit more confidence and persistence will ensure that the conversation stays in the right language.

14. I'll Always Have an Accent

Way too much emphasis is put on speaking with no accent, as if being a spy is the ultimate point of your language project rather than communicating with other human beings. Having a little accent can be quite charming. Believe me, it doesn't hinder communication.

Even if you may always have an accent, this is no reason not to pour everything into this project so that you can be a genuinely fluent speaker. Speaking perfectly is impossible, because even native speakers make mistakes. And native speakers have interesting and varied accents too!

Accent reduction is possible, though, and something we'll discuss later.

15. My Friends and Family Won't Support Me

When I decided to get serious with my Spanish, after almost six months of speaking only English while in the country, I thought my friends would instantly support me. Unfortunately, this wasn't the case. Some of my Spanish friends, it turns out, had been using me to get free English practice. Some of my English-speaking friends fluent in Spanish didn't have the patience to help me and would only speak back to me in English rather than supporting my efforts to practice my Spanish.

Many of us will go through this difficulty. Our friends or family may not offer any support—language-related or moral—to help us with this huge challenge.

There is no simple one-size-fits-all solution to this problem. But the first thing you should do is to tell your friends and family that you are passionate about learning a new language and you genuinely need their support. They might not appreciate how seriously dedicated you are to learning the language. They might have thought it was just a silly hobby. Showing them how serious you are might convince them to give you the support you need.

And if you still have trouble getting the support you need from those closest to you, remember there are huge communities of people online and in your city who will share in your passion for language learning—even native speakers themselves—so that you can always find support, even if it isn't from the friends you already have.

16. Everybody Speaks English

If you're a tourist hopping between five-star hotels or sticking to the well-beaten tourist trail in particular countries, you can indeed get by without learning the local language. Expensive restaurants provide an English translation of their menus, overpriced tour guides herd you along the same route many millions of other foreigners have traveled, while talking excellent English, and when you board your flight home, at least one of the airline attendants will speak wonderful English to you, no matter where you are flying from.

This is incredibly limiting, though. The prominence of English prevents you from getting off the beaten track and chatting with people who don't cater to tourists.

While I was traveling through China, for instance, many of the staff at the hotels didn't speak English. An expression of concern always appeared on their faces as I, a white foreigner, approached them—until, of course, I started speaking Mandarin.

Even if you can get by in other countries speaking only English, you'll also miss out on a lot. Learning the local language opens up so many doors, from finding cheap local rates to hanging out with people who have never had the chance to speak to foreigners. It allows you to see the true culture of a local place, rather than a cookie-cutter packaged version. And it's all thanks to *not speaking English*.

TALKING TRUMPS TECHNOLOGY

People often bring up automatic translation with me. On a few occasions, people have even suggested that they can shove their smartphones in someone's face to figure out what that person is saying. Presto! All communication problems will be solved.

While technology does advance at an incredible rate, I can definitely say that learning a new language will never, ever be replaced by technology. Even if in, say, fifty or a hundred years' time the technology is there to provide accurate subtitles on your iContactLenses as a person speaks, people will still want to interact with a human being through language. You can't live through translations. You have to deal with the language directly. So much of human communication is about

context, reading complex body language, and understanding
the subtle meaning of pauses and volume to gauge someone's
feelings. This is incredibly hard to emulate with a computer.

17. I Can't Keep Up with Other People's Progress

There is a major problem in comparing ourselves to others—the
others we think have it so easy only let us see what they decide
to reveal about themselves. When they share their stories and
fail to share details about any bumps they've encountered on
their journeys, it can seem like they have it easy and are much
smarter than we are, that we are puny in comparison to such
immense giants.

Every successful language learner has had many challenges,
failures, and frustrations along the road to fluency and beyond.
If someone ever thinks I had it easy, I like to remind that person
that I barely passed German in school, couldn't speak Spanish
despite living there for six months, and could barely string
together even the most basic sentences in Irish, even after ten
years of schooling. Each language I've taken on has presented
me with new challenges, and the same is true for every other
successful language learner. We all face our own challenges.

Successful language learners continue on *despite* the challenges. That's the difference. When you come to a challenge,
rather than thinking, *I might as well give up because that successful*
language learner didn't have to deal with this, ask yourself, *What*

would that successful language learner do to get around this challenge if faced with it? You may be surprised to find out that this person faced a very similar, if not the same, challenge at some point in the past. And even if he or she didn't, many other ultimately successful learners have.

18. Failure Begets Failure

If you've tried to learn a language before and failed, then you might have concluded you're bad at language learning. (I'm hoping the points I've made so far are emphasizing how untrue this is!) The much more logical conclusion is that you were learning the language in a way that was wrong for you.

There is no one true or perfect approach to language learning that is universally applicable to everyone. The traditional academic approach, which so many of us have passed through, simply does not work for many learners. Then again, there are those who have successfully learned with that approach. It's not that there are smart and dumb learners or universally good and bad learning systems, but there are systems that may work well for particular people and (many!) systems that may work poorly for others. The trick is to experiment and see what works for you. You may try something that doesn't produce results for you, and if that's the case, discard it and try something else.

Try a few of the suggestions in this book and see if they work for you. If they don't, that's okay. Experiment with alternative language learning techniques online, many of which I'll be discussing and providing links to in chapter summaries. From this, you can come up with your own ways to learn. The trick is to keep trying until you find a way that produces real results for you. It's never *you* who's broken, but your current approach. Fix the approach, discard what doesn't work, and you will be much more successful.

However, sometimes the issue isn't a general one with a one-size-fits-all solution, but a specific problem with the language you are learning. Should you learn an Arabic dialect or MSA? Where can you find good resources for learning the Irish language? Why does this language have to have masculine and feminine (or neuter and common, etc.) nouns? What's the deal with putting the letter *a* before every person's name or reference to them in certain Spanish sentences?

These kinds of specific language questions are challenges that may slow you down, but there are always answers. I cover a few points about individual languages in chapter 6, though I barely scratch the surface, but if you run into an issue with your language, just ask someone about it. Not all answers are covered in books; sometimes another person with experience in the language can give you a whole new perspective on that issue.

For instance, you can ask a question about pretty much any issue in the very active Fluent in 3 Months online forum (fi3m .com/forum), where I or another active language learner will give you some suggestions.

Otherwise, find a helpful native speaker and ask that person directly. Most questions do have an answer. Sometimes you can find that answer quickly enough in a book- or web-based language course, but you'll always get the best, most useful answer by asking a human being.

19. Once I Forget a Language, I Can't Relearn It

People who used to speak a different language when they were young but never fully picked it up often feel they let a golden opportunity slip through their fingers. But it's really just a case of rebooting their efforts and starting fresh with that language until they get it back.

One of my blog readers, Anna Fodor, shared her inspirational story with us. Born and raised in England, she grew up with a Czech mother and a Slovak father. So she should have grown up trilingual, right? Not quite. She spoke Czech up until the age of four and then stopped speaking it when she entered school. Her mother would speak to her in Czech and she'd reply in English, until her mother eventually stopped trying to communicate with her daughter in her native tongue.

Finally, when Anna went to university, she decided to reboot her efforts with Czech. She really enjoyed it, and it helped her realize all the aspects of Czech she *didn't* know. She had assumed the Czech part of her brain had been somehow locked away in her mind.

After graduation, she moved to Prague with the aim of learning to speak Czech. This was a pretty vague aim for her, but soon after arriving in Prague, she found my blog and my constant nudges for people to just *speak* the language, despite any mistakes. She had been looking for a magic solution to her problems for years, but now she needed to put in the work.

So one day she decided to stop overanalyzing things and just started speaking Czech with her mother. It was hard, and she was so scared that her mother would criticize her mistakes. But to her surprise, her mother exclaimed, "Wow, your Czech is almost perfect! This was really amazing. We've just had a real fluent conversation together!"

Anna's Czech wasn't quite "perfect," but her mother's words—in Czech—meant so much to her that she almost cried. It was like having a huge weight of childhood trauma lifted. She continues improving her Czech, but she's learned that it's never too late to get into a language, and she will strive for fluency, while being proud of the fact that she has already achieved her main goal of being able to truly converse with her mother.

20. Disabilities Make It Impossible to Learn a New Language

This is a rough one, because it can be frustrating when we have unfairly been dealt a real, medically confirmed disadvantage as language learners.

When this issue comes up, I am reminded of Julie Ferguson's story. Julie is severely deaf and partially blind. Despite this, incredibly, she has still managed to learn five languages as well as the basics of several others.

Her parents realized that she had a hearing problem when she was two years old. She had to go to speech therapy and had difficulty producing consonants like s, h, and f. Over the years, she has learned to get around her hearing difficulties by lipreading and extrapolating from what she *does* hear.

When her older brother—who has the same condition she does—started high school, she became aware of foreign languages and was really excited to get started on them herself. She turned up to her first French class with glee, but she finished it in a flood of tears. Her teacher didn't know about her hearing problem, and the lesson had been given entirely as an oral one with no written cues. Since then, though, Julie has learned to always ask for new words to be written down for her.

Despite this bad start, Julie went on to study French for four years in high school plus one year in university. She also took three years of Spanish. She would shine at the written word in both languages, but listening was her sticking point.

Since her brother had gone down the same path, ahead of her, she found out that she could request both her French and Spanish listening examinations be done with a real person reading the script to her, which allowed her to lip-read as well as listen. Her teachers in school were otherwise very encouraging and supportive, and she ended up winning prizes for being the best French *and* Spanish student in her fourth year.

During university, she had the chance to study for a year in Sweden. She made sure that her teacher knew about her hearing problems from the start, and she was now much more confident about asking for things to be repeated or written down. She also grew more confident about using Swedish in front of others without much embarrassment.

By the end of university, she had learned three languages. Since then, she has studied basic Gaelic and even recently started learning Japanese. In just a few months, despite how difficult her condition makes it for her, she learned the meaning of hundreds of kanji (Japanese characters) and even started speaking Japanese.

Julie is a true testament to the idea that there are no limits to what a motivated person can achieve. She has haggled for French books in a street market in France. She has shopped for tea in Sweden and even used her Swedish to "hack" Norwegian and Danish while traveling in Norway and Denmark. Her passion for language learning has also meant that she has reserved restaurant tables in Italian, bought coffee in Greek, and spent over half an hour discussing, in Spanish, the state of the world with a little old lady in Barcelona.

Rather than live up to people's stereotypes of how she should live her life, she has been the one helping others during her travels, translating for other students, friends, and even teachers, as they were too afraid to do it or hadn't learned the language themselves.

Most Myths Are Just Excuses

"Whether you think you can,
or you think you can't—you're right."

—HENRY FORD

Language learning is a mentally challenging endeavor. As such, if we're sure we can't, then we lose our motivation, our passion dwindles, our pessimism takes over, and we simply won't learn the language. This is not due to any reason we give but our devotion to that reason.

I hope you see from the previous stories that no matter what challenges you face, someone else has gone through the same or much worse. If Julie has the courage to take on so many languages, then how can you fall back on such weak excuses as being too busy or not having a language gene?

The truth is that passion will get you through every problem if you are serious about learning a language. There is no excuse good enough to justify not being able to learn a language. If you didn't find the reason holding you back among the twenty I listed, however, it may in fact have an entire chapter dedicated to it later. And if you are still in doubt about a particular setback that prevents you from learning a language, check out fi3m.com/ch-1 and find an even longer version of this list, watch some inspiring videos, and read stories from other struggling language learners and suggestions on where you can go for language advice. No matter what problem you may be facing, someone before you has had the same problem yet has learned the target language regardless.

Momentum is essential to both beginning and maintaining good progress in language learning, which is why I wanted to start by clearing these major hurdles. Too many language learners focus on the content of a language and on finding the right courses, but even those who have great language learning tools and strategies are still at a disadvantage if they don't clear these hurdles first.

Now that we've got the right attitude and extinguished as many excuses as possible, we can charge into this language learning project with much greater momentum.

CHAPTER 2

Your Mission,
Should You Choose to Accept It

*Do away with vague daydreams,
such as "learn Spanish," by setting specific end goals
within specific time frames and incorporating new
language learning techniques to achieve
concrete results.*

The most common time of the year, by far, to decide to take on a new language is of course January 1, as part of a New Year's resolution. Generally, the resolution is something along the lines of "Learn Spanish (or whatever language it may be) within a year." Unfortunately, many fail miserably. This is precisely why I recommend you pick a specific target with a specific deadline for your language learning project. I don't have resolutions; I have missions. The word *mission* even has a sense of urgency and requires a plan of action beyond what simply promising yourself ever could. Having watched probably too many action movies and

TV shows while growing up, I like to add a little drama to otherwise mundane tasks, and the concept of a mission to be completed against a ticking clock makes it seem much more exciting.

This brings us to the title of this book: *Fluent in 3 Months*. The point is not that you have to aim for fluency in three months, but that you do need to be specific about what you're aiming for, and this title is one such example of a very specific target and a deadline to reach it by. Successful language learners are those who are as specific as possible with their goals.

To help you gauge what to aim for, I'll dive into what *fluency* and other useful targets really mean, and we'll look at how much time you need to reach those targets. Plus, I'll explain why "Fluent in 3 Months" has been a great goal for me personally and why fluency—and beyond—is a goal more of us can strive for.

What Fluency Isn't

The question of what fluency means is one of great controversy, depending on whom you ask. I want to provide a much more precise understanding of fluency once and for all.

First, some definitions can be way too loose. A monolingual novice with next to no language learning experience may ask me which languages I speak fluently, but before I quantify my answer I will ask for her understanding of the idea of fluency, because her definition may be more what I'd consider that of a *functional tourist*—a level easily achievable by anyone within a few hours or days—and not fluency at all.

Second, there is sometimes a too elitist way of looking at being fluent (or saying that you "speak" a language) as being equivalent to a native speaker in all ways. People who look at fluency this way sometimes go overboard and demand that you should be able to

- participate in a debate on a complex or philosophical topic,

- speak with no hesitations,

- use complex vocabulary and advanced expressions,

- never have any serious miscommunications, and

- be able to participate in a discussion that any typical native might have.

The problem here, though, is that if you have such high criteria for fluency, then I have to confess I am not fluent even in English, my native language!

I can't participate in a debate on many complex topics (including philosophical ones; it's just not my forte). I hesitate all the time in English (watch any unscripted video of me speaking English online, and you'll hear plenty of ums and uhs). I am not the kind of person to use pompous vocabulary in everyday conversations, or even in formal ones. And because I'm Irish, I have had to learn to adjust the way I speak and the words I use whenever I'm with Americans or other foreign native-English speakers.

Finally, I can't participate in any conversation a typical native might have. If you start talking soccer (or any sport, for that matter), which I don't follow, you'll lose me quickly. Many guys can talk sports for hours, but I'm just not that interested, so I can't join in. If you start talking about nice fashionable clothes, which many native English-speaking women can do fine, I'm a dunce and can't contribute. I almost never watch TV in English anymore, so if you start talking about the latest show everyone is crazy for, I'm going to be able to offer nothing more than defeated shrugs.

These aren't necessarily complex conversations, and they are conversations many typical natives with no specialization or advanced studies can participate in, but I can't because I'm not either interested in or familiar with the topics.

So if you had these criteria for fluency in the past, discard them immediately, because this is effectively saying that you have to be able to do in your target language what you can't even do in your native language, which is a totally unfair and unrealistic standard to set for yourself.

What Fluency Is

Let's look at a more formal definition, from the *Oxford English Dictionary:*

> **fluent** adjective: (of a person) able to express oneself easily and articulately; able to speak or write a particular foreign

language easily and accurately; (of a foreign language) spoken accurately and with facility.

I don't see any implication here that you have to pass yourself off as a native speaker or never make mistakes. Speaking a language accurately and with facility is precisely what I have in mind when I aim for fluency.

However, this is not something you will ever get a consensus on. There is no absolute, discernible point you pass when you can say, "Now I speak the language fluently." It's like the idea of beauty, in that way. You can have more of it, but there is no threshold you finally cross that signals you've arrived. It's all relative.

This is a problem if we want something distinct to aim for, though. And even if we each came up with a personal understanding of what feels accurate or good enough, because we are all filled with bias, confidence issues, unrealistic expectations, and elitist standards, as well as definitions of the word *fluent* that might be way too flexible, I don't think such vague understandings are useful for a mission with a specific target.

The CEFRL System

With such conflicting ideas about what constitutes fluency, the system I rely on is a much more scientific and well-established language threshold criterion used by the major bodies that examine language levels in Europe. Foundations like the Alliance

Française, the Instituto Cervantes, and the Goethe-Institut all use the Common European Framework of Reference for Languages (CEFRL), a comprehensive guideline of language evaluation.

This system uses standard terminology, accepted across Europe (and used by many institutions for Asian languages, even if not adopted by those countries formally), for specific language levels. In the terminology, basically A means beginner, B means intermediate, and C means advanced. Each level is then split into lower 1 and upper 2. So upper beginner level is A2, and lower advanced level would be C1. The six levels on this scale, from the simplest to the most complex, are A1, A2, B1, B2, C1, and C2.

On this scale, an A level is what I would generally call a functional tourist: good enough to get by for basic necessities, or a beginner in various stages. C level implies mastery: you can work in the language exactly as you would in your native tongue and are effectively as good as a native in all ways, though you may still have an accent.

In my mind, fluency starts at level B2 and includes all levels above it (C1 and C2). More specifically, a person who reaches the B2 level on the CEFRL scale, relevant to the conversational aspect, is defined as someone who

> **can interact with a degree of fluency and spontaneity that makes regular interaction with native speakers quite possible without strain for either party.**

This means that, for a solid fluency goal, you should aim to participate in regular conversations without strain for either you or the people you are speaking with. That's regular conversations, not debates on sixteenth-century French politics.

For me, B2 fluency—at least in a conversational, social context—implies that I can live my life in this language exactly as I would in English. I can go to any social event that I would typically go to in English and chat with natives without having them slow down for my benefit. I can discuss anything I would in English at a casual event, and natives can generally talk to me as they would with another native speaker.

What it doesn't imply is also very important to consider. Hesitations are okay, and accents are fine. (In fact, you can earn a C2 diploma with an accent, as long as it doesn't hinder communication.) Also fine at the B2 level is the inability to discuss some very complex topics.

Realizing your limitations is essential, because aiming for perfection is a fool's errand. You need to be realistic, but you can also aim for the milestone on your path of maybe someday "mastering" a language. There is never an end point at which you can say your work in learning the language is done. Even in my native language of English I still encounter new words and aspects of other dialects I didn't know before. Learning a language can be a lifelong adventure, but the point is that you can reach certain stages within finite times when you have those stages well defined.

Even if you don't agree with my specific definition of fluency, make sure your definition is as clear as possible and includes specifics of what it is *not*.

How Much Time Do You Need to Reach Fluency?

Now, as you read previously, you can have a particular milestone in mind to aim for—advanced beginner (A2), conversational (B1), fluent (B2), mastery (C2), or others—but here comes the big question: How long does it take to get there?

This book, of course, suggests that you can become fluent in three months, but fluency won't be achieved if you don't do the work! You have to live up to your side of the bargain—you have to put in the time and stick to the plan. Also, the process requires a lot of strategic mental and emotional adjustments. It's very hard, for example, to realistically become fluent in three months if this is your first-ever language learning project.

Generally, I would recommend you aim for *conversational* (level B1 on the CEFRL scale) or *advanced beginner* (level A2) in three months. In the process, you'll discover tweaks you'll need to make to your learning approach in order for it to work best for you. If you succeed in learning one language to fluency over a longer period, then your approach may be ready for you to use in a shorter—say, three-month—period of time on your next language.

An intensive language learning project demands your absolute focus. But if you're serious about learning a particular language, you will always make the time and give it several hours a day, even if you work full-time.

Ultimately, languages are learned in hours, not months or years. It's not about the amount of time that passes from the moment you begin the project, but the amount of time you put into it. Whether or not your process adds up to a huge number of hours, the only thing worth counting is the time when you are 100 percent focused on learning, living, and using the language. To realistically expect to make good progress in a language in a short amount of time, you have to put at least two hours a day into it, and ideally more. As mentioned in the previous chapter, you can always make the time, even if it's a few minutes a day, to advance. But you have to set aside much more than scattered study sessions if you want to advance quickly. Do what it takes to create this time, avoid other side projects, and fill your language learning slot every day. If you put just a few hours a week into it, fluency in three months is indeed impossible.

There's no magic fluency number either. You can't multiply eight hours (the number of hours a day you would theoretically have available if you could work on the language full-time) by ninety days to figure out how long it will take you to learn a new language. You simply have to put in as much work as you can, as intensively as you can, with as much emphasis on solving immediate language problems as you possibly can in order to progress. If you do, you will quickly see how much time is necessary for you to advance to a higher level.

So why am I so crazy about three months? The answer is incredibly simple: that's all the time I've had during many of my projects. When I would go to a new country to learn the language, the visa limit for tourists was about three months. Fortunately for me, that's the amount of time I usually liked to spend in a foreign country before moving on to a new one. So I had only three months to reach my deadline. It's as simple as that.

Even though I no longer go to a country to learn a language, and I now prefer to learn in advance of traveling abroad, I have found that three months is as good a time line as any. It's long enough to realistically aim for a high fluency goal but short enough that the goal is always within sight, that three-month deadline pressuring you to work harder.

When we make a resolution—such as a New Year's resolution—with a vague deadline of learning a language within a year, or to speak it fluently "someday," even the best of us can get lazy. There are seven days in a week, and "someday" is not one of them.

When you give yourself a short deadline, rather than thinking you have plenty of time, you tend to work as efficiently as possible. Deadlines of one, three, or six months are excellent for this reason. Even if you're more interested in a year deadline, break that year into smaller achievable chunks.

You don't have to pick three months for your major end goal; I've also had missions of "conversational in one to two months" and "get by as a confident tourist in a few weeks," but my successes have more often been with a three-month time line.

If three months feels right to you, focus on one project and have an adventurous end goal. You don't have to pick fluency, but look at that CEFRL table (fi3m.com/cefrl) and see which level would be enough of a challenge to truly push you but still be realistic, given the time you can put in.

Various Grades of Success

Remember that language is a means to communicate. The only way you can fail is if you don't try to communicate at all. And the only way you can fail in your language learning mission is if you are at exactly the same point at the end of your first mission as you were at the start.

I've missed my goals plenty of times. When I moved to Taiwan, for instance, I aimed for fluency in Mandarin in three months, but I didn't reach it. Was my Mandarin, and the entire project, therefore a waste of time? No. I actually reached B1 (conversational, which was checked independently by the Live the Language [LTL] Mandarin School in Beijing). As long as a person spoke slowly to me or rephrased what he or she had said, I could socialize. I wasn't fluent, but I was conversant. And I was really proud of this. Thanks to that intensive project, I can continue to speak Mandarin for the rest of my life, and I have a fantastic new place to start from as I strive toward fluency and beyond.

With language learning there is no true failure if you can communicate with other human beings. However, you should always strive for the highest grade of possible success. If you can "only" speak conversationally, rather than fluently, after your intensive three months, you have still successfully learned how to communicate with another person in a new language, which will inspire you to take your language skills to the next level.

However, be careful not to use the "even small successes count" perspective as a crutch to rationalize slacking off. Be sure to push yourself outside your comfort zone. If the goal you've set for yourself has a 100 percent chance of success, then frankly you aren't aiming high enough.

Mini-Missions

Mini-missions, as I like to call them, take on the absolute biggest specific problem you may have at a particular moment with a language and help you focus on solving that problem as quickly as possible.

For instance, when I started studying Mandarin there were, of course, many things to learn, and I found that when I tried to use phrases from my phrase book, people didn't understand me. My tones were way off. Because of this, my mini-mission—my absolute priority—was to focus on getting my tones right. I focused only on tones, not on vocabulary or reading Chinese script or any number of other things—just tones. I didn't "solve" this problem in my first week, but I did become easier to understand when I spoke. Once my tones were in good enough shape, I was ready to tackle basic vocabulary.

By week two, my biggest problem was that I relied too much on my phrase book. I needed to work on saying things spontaneously, from memory. So I tackled this issue as a mini-mission, and soon enough I was able to speak several phrases from memory, and I continued with this pattern of setting mini-missions for myself throughout the project.

These mini-missions give you a very real—and earned—feeling of accomplishment and progress. They are specific plans of action that fit your particular language needs precisely and help you deal right away with your most immediate challenges. This helps you focus on each challenge until you conquer it, while also helping you make huge strides toward the bigger goal a few months down the road. As an example, rather than assigning myself a vague weeklong mission to learn Mandarin vocabulary, I made sure I processed sixty flash cards a day with the specific intention of learning how to order food while traveling freely around a new country.

At the end of my first month learning Mandarin, I felt I had reached something of a plateau. I could have basic touristy exchanges from memory and with passable tones, but these exchanges lasted only ten to fifteen seconds. I couldn't have an actual conversation. So I gave myself a brain-melting mini-mission. As the name implies, *brain-melting* forces you to think fast, try to extrapolate what you're hearing, and remember vocabulary, all while processing the context for clues. During the week following that first month, I scheduled time to sit down with native speakers for hour-long conversations.

What a week! But at the end of it, I had practiced so much that I could hold a conversation for several minutes. These weren't complex conversations—I mostly described what I did that day—but this is exactly the point of a mini-mission. I had successfully forced myself outside my comfort zone and, in the process, figured out how to talk for several minutes and understand a native speaker's questions beyond my limited range. Plus, since I had only one goal and one mini-mission, it was a lot easier to tailor my work specifically to make this happen.

I remember when I was beginning to learn a little Hungarian, and I received my first phone call in that language. I couldn't rely on visual cues, as I tend to do in the early stages, and the call quality wasn't all that great. I had to think fast and attempt to get information out of the caller. After that very short one- to two-minute call, I felt exhausted. I could almost feel my brain being pushed into overdrive. Since then, I've added phone or Skype calls to my mini-mission itineraries.

Through brain-melting mini-missions like these, you can push on to a new language level. If you don't try several brain-melting sessions throughout your project, then you're simply not pushing yourself hard enough. Learning a new language should certainly be fun and enjoyable, but pushing through the frustrating parts determines whether or not you'll reach the next level. You have to move out of your comfort zone. And the mini-missions are designed to do just that.

Focus on your biggest issue and tackle it. It will be hard (that's why it's your biggest issue!) but get through it, go headfirst into frustration, and, like tearing off a bandage, you will come out on the other side happy that you got it over with quickly.

Burnout

For those of you taking on this project full-time, there's a catch. If your entire project is made up of brain-melting moments, you can burn out incredibly quickly. Unfortunately, burnout is one of the biggest reasons people give up on learning a language entirely.

At first, I thought three full months of focused learning would be the ideal amount of time to reach my target, without any breaks at all to speak English. What I eventually figured out, though, was that I could only keep up this kind of active, intense learning for about three weeks. After three weeks, I couldn't retain anything else for about a week. I reached a saturation point. If you have greater endurance than little old me, then perhaps you can keep on going, but I think most people realistically reach a burnout point.

Absolute full-time immersion and pushing yourself as much as I suggest require you also take breaks. Since discovering this, I have found that working full-time all week on a language, then giving myself one evening off each week to socialize in another language, helps me recharge my batteries and, ultimately, work the most effectively.

Once a month I would also take an entire weekend off the language project and hang out with other foreigners like myself, go for a swim, dance for a few hours—anything not related to the language I was learning. I got great mileage out of this while doing my Arabic learning project in Brazil, as well as my most recent one, to learn Japanese in Spain.

Breaks like this are also an effective psychological tool. I had weekly goals and then "rewarded" myself with a break just after (hopefully) reaching those goals, and I gave myself much longer breaks after achieving any much larger monthly objectives. Breaks are essential during a full-time immersion project. Use them to recharge your batteries and as motivation to work harder to reach a specific milestone.

Frustrating moments are inevitable. To keep them to a minimum, try to have fun with your language every day. Assign yourself language tasks that you actually look forward to. Reward yourself after studying several dozen flash cards, for instance, by watching a few minutes of a silly soap opera in the language you're studying or reading a comic book in that same language. When it doesn't feel like work, you can accomplish so much more.

Plan of Action

Discipline is choosing between
what you want now and what you want most.

All the best ideas in the world are worth nothing if they aren't implemented. That's why you absolutely need to have a plan of action. Before you get started on your project, be sure to keep these points in mind:

- Decide precisely what you are aiming for. Have a look at a more detailed explanation of the various levels of the CEFRL system at fi3m.com/cefrl and decide which would be slightly higher than a safe target for you, so you really push yourself. Pay careful attention to both what is required and what is *not* required at that level.

- Set aside a specific period, whether it is one, three, or six months, and make sure your language learning project is your highest priority during this time.

- During your intensive learning project, make sure to focus on the biggest issue you have and try to solve it, or greatly reduce it, with mini-missions rather than going through a generic course, which may not be well suited to the precise point you are aiming for.

- If you do take on this project full-time, make sure to take breaks so you don't burn yourself out.

- Announce your mission to the world, which establishes a chain of accountability since your friends and family will then be aware of your goals and can follow along with your progress. You can do this with Facebook status updates, a blog, or your own log on the Fluent in 3 Months forum at fi3m.com/forum.

With all obstacles cleared, and a good plan of action for where you aim to be throughout your language learning project, it's time to start looking at the tools that will allow you to accomplish this project. The first one is the memory to absorb all that new vocabulary!

For more thoughts on language missions and other topics relevant to this chapter, check out fi3m.com/ch–2.

CHAPTER 3

How to Learn Thousands of Words Quickly

> If you don't have the memory of a supercomputer, don't worry. This chapter explains why we forget things and teaches a much more efficient—and fun—way to remember foreign words.

One of the most intimidating aspects of learning a language is the huge amount of vocabulary that lies ahead of you. Depending on how you count them, a language could have as many as a half a million words. Surely that's too many for someone without a savant's memory to handle.

Well, considering that over half the population of the planet speaks more than one language, this of course can't be true. There are several shortcuts and tricks to help you absorb many words a lot more quickly than you think you're able to, even if you're the kind of person (like me) who still forgets where he left his keys!

In this chapter, I want to focus exclusively on making sure you have no trouble quickly accessing the many words and phrases required to speak a language, and that you never again use the excuse of having a "terrible memory."

Rote Rehearsal: Why the Memorization We're Taught in School Doesn't Work

One thing that, to this day, still boggles my mind is that we learn so many facts in school, but we never really learn how to learn.

In ancient Greece, the idea of memorizing through associative techniques (like mnemonics) was actually quite normal, but this was replaced in modern times with . . . well, nothing really.

Ancient Greeks had fantastic memories, because there were no textbooks or notepads to take home with them. Most people were illiterate and, regardless, "paper" was very expensive. Lectures were oral, and people came up with clever ways of remembering poems, stories, and any long spoken passages.

Later, the widespread availability of books meant that anyone could look up something in print whenever he or she needed to, so memorizing became less common and less relevant. We have an even more pronounced version of this nowadays: many people end up not learning, or even memorizing, any facts, since they can always Google them in an instant.

This is unfortunate, as it doesn't push our minds to their fullest potentials. We no longer seem able to efficiently hold information in our memories but instead refer to a printed or online source.

What replaced the mnemonic techniques of the ancient Greeks was basically a system of repetitive exposure to information with the presumption it will eventually "sink in." For instance, when I was learning German in school and came across a new word, such as *der Tisch* (meaning "the table"), since I didn't know what else to do, the only way I saw to assimilate this word was through rote memorization. That is to say, I repeated over and over in my head: "*der Tisch*, the table, *der Tisch*, the table, *der Tisch*, the table." After saying it a few dozen times, it would kind of sink in, and I'd remember it a little. But the next day, or a few days later, it would be gone. What was "table" in German again?

I find that rote memorization is somewhat useful for *recognizing* words. So after a few dozen—or a few hundred—repetitions, I might (for a short period) remember what *der Tisch* is, if I were to read it. But it's not symmetrical (meaning, it's not a word I can both recognize and produce), so I'm out of luck if I want to produce words myself, and the speaking part of language acquisition is much harder for most of us than simply recognizing words spoken or read. This is another reason my "speak from day one" suggestion seems absurd to so many people.

Even for recognizing words, rote memorization doesn't burn a word into your memory as you might think it would. What really keeps it there? We make memories by association. Sights, smells, strange and powerful images, stories, and the like are what make the most memorable events in our lives stand out. Repetition works too, but it's only effective when you have a lot of repetition, and that can get incredibly tedious when you deal with so many words on an individual level.

So scrap rote rehearsal, and let's have a look at two approaches that have been more effective for many language learners.

The Keyword Method for Learning Words Quickly

A much more effective, and much more fun, method of learning vocabulary is through associating very visual images with something that sounds like the word you want to remember, also known as the *keyword method*.

You need to create an amusing, animated, and unforgettable image, or even a short story, whenever you come across a new word or phrase you want to remember in order to stick it to something in your mind. These images or keywords are much easier to recall, both when attempting to recognize a word and when producing a word yourself.

To show you how effective this is, I'll jump straight into giving several examples:

Gare

First, let's look at the French word for "train station": *gare* (pronounced with an *ah* sound). When I saw this word for the first time, I tried to think of a word similar to it in English. The closest word that came to me, which at least starts with the *gar* sound, was "Garfield" (the popular comic strip cat, who even has his own movie). This is a great word to use because Garfield is a very visual and funny image, as he's a fat, lazy, sarcastic orange cat.

To be more visual with the English translation, rather than think of a generic train station (very easy to forget!), make your image one from a cartoon, a TV show, or a place you have fond memories of. When I was learning French, I got nostalgic about my time in Valencia, Spain, and visiting the city's main train station to go on fun excursions to the countryside. So I picked *that* train station, visualizing it clearly in my mind.

Now combine the two in the most ridiculous way possible. Garfield couldn't simply be sitting in the train station, as that image was far too easily forgettable. I imagined the train station on a very busy day, and then suddenly Garfield comes bursting through the doors with a suitcase, panting (since he's so out of shape), and people turn around and look at this strange sight, but he has no time for them. He runs up to the timetable, sweating like crazy while he looks for the train to Bologna—the city he is going to for the world lasagna-eating championship. He gasps when he sees that his train is about to leave. He dashes to the right platform, only to catch sight of the train pulling out already. He runs after it, puffing frantically, throws his suitcase in one of the back compartments, jumps in after it, and makes it just in time.

This ridiculous story is one that is much harder to forget. The precise details of it are not so important, except for the fact that it's definitely Garfield who is performing all the actions, and it's definitely happening in a train station. This means that later, when you see the word *gare* in some random French text, you can go through the thought process: *gare* sounds like "Garfield" . . . and Garfield was in the train station.

Conversely—and something much more useful than you'll ever get from rote memorization—when you need to say "train station" in French, you imagine your favorite train station (Valencia's, in my case), think of what interesting thing happened there, and you suddenly can't avoid seeing that silly orange cat running through it. If Garfield is running through a train station, then "train station" in French must be *gare*!

The recall process takes less than a second and barely slows down a nicely flowing conversation. The memory of the word is easily accessible and comes to you much more quickly than the digging you'd have to do with rote memorization.

Mùbiāo

Now let's take a look at a Chinese word. One that I needed often was the word that meant "target" or "goal," because I frequently discussed my fluency goal in Chinese when asked why I was in Taiwan. Since I wasn't learning the writing system yet, all I needed to do was learn the sound of the word, which is *mùbiāo* (falling tone on *mù*, and first tone, which doesn't go up or down but remains steady, on *biāo*).

So how do you learn this while incorporating the tone? Like anything else, it just requires a bit of imagination. Think about it for a second yourself: What would you come up with from *mù* (pronounced *moo*) and then *biǎo* (*bee-ow*)? I don't know about you, but I thought of a cow, then a bee, and then simply the *ow* (as in "ouch") sound from pain.

Next, it's a case of throwing ideas out there. It doesn't matter how silly, nonsensical, politically incorrect, sexual, or personal your story is, as long as it stands out in your memory. This is the short story that I came up with for this word:

I'm walking through a field with a bow and arrow in the early evening as the sun is setting. I want to practice my shooting skills, but I don't see something challenging to aim at. Suddenly a cow falls from the sky: "Mmmooooooo" (crash).

She stumbles to find her footing, and I see my opportunity. Conveniently, a bull's-eye of concentric red and white circles has been pre-painted on her rear end, and I position myself by kneeling a little so my bow is at the same height as the poor cow's ass.

This is no ordinary bow and arrow, though. My arrow is made entirely of bees. I pull it back and launch it to fly horizontally through the air, and since I positioned myself correctly, it flies straight into the target and goes up the cow's bum! The poor animal forgets herself and rather than moo, she can't resist yelling a loud "Ow!"

(No cows or bees were harmed in the making of this mnemonic.)

While it's true this story takes a few minutes to write out, our brains work much faster when verbalizing (or writing) isn't necessary. All I need from this story are the essentials: "target" is *moo* (falling tone) and *bee-ow* (first tone, level—as in the story where the arrow is shot straight at the same height as the target). Also, when you hear *mùbiāo*, you know it means "target," which is symmetrical, so I can both recognize it *and* produce it.

Some details are treated differently; for instance, the falling tone in Chinese doesn't actually sound like someone falling and is more like a stern "No!" than a dramatic movie "Noooooo!" but when I was learning Chinese I made a visual aspect of my mnemonics that incorporates these movements so I could also remember the tones.

Even forgetting the tones (which I discuss in more detail in chapter 6), can you see how with a language as distant from English as Mandarin there is still hope, if you have a good imagination?

Other Examples

I could fill a whole book just with some of the craziest keyword-association stories I've come up with. But here are some random ones to give you further inspiration:

- *Playa* in Spanish means "beach." For this, I imagined a cheesy pickup artist (a "player") strolling down a beach I know well, trying to pick up pretty Spanish girls but getting slapped in the face; to give the story a comedic effect, the slaps made it easier to remember.

- The German example I began the chapter with, *der Tisch*—this word to me sounds like the start of the word "tissue." So I imagine trying to sit down to dinner at a table made entirely out of tissues, which collapses as soon as I put my bowl of soup on it. The soup then spills all over the floor and a little on me . . . so then I have to mop it up with all the tissues I have!

- The Czech word *prvni* looks and sounds nothing like any English word I can think of, but it's an important word to learn since it means "first." For this, I inserted a few vowels to make it easier and came up with "pro van." I imagined a very complex scene of me winning the "professional van Olympics," driving up into "first" place on the podium in my strange-looking white van, crying as I am handed my bouquet of flowers and the medal is placed around my neck, while I remain in the driver's seat. "Pro van" is easy to remember from this scene and, with a little repetition, you'll be able to instantly recall *prvni*.

These examples are all nouns (things). To expand on them and remember verbs (action words), adjectives (description words like "big," "red," "closed," etc.), and adverbs ("quickly," "happily"), you can still use a noun to make the connection.

For instance, to remember that *verde* (pronounced somewhat like *bird-ay,* which itself sounds like "birdie") is "green" in

Spanish, I imagined green grass. The first thing that comes to mind with the adjective "green" is, of course, grass, which suddenly transforms into millions of cute green birdies flocking into the air and leaving the field as nothing but soil, when it was so beautiful and green before.

How Can You Come Up with These Associations?

When I suggest coming up with such keyword associations, a retort I immediately hear from people is that they take far too much time and are much too complicated. It slows you down to go through the whole story every time you need to recall a word, but eventually you don't have to go through the whole story.

When I first tried this approach, I found myself creating an association for a new word more slowly than I would have liked. After a week or so of doing this consistently, my mind and imagination expanded to come up with good images quickly.

At first, my examples were boring and far from memorable. Or, if they were good, it took me an entire minute or more to come up with it, which is a lot of time when you are dealing with a long list of words to memorize. In a very short time, though, my childlike imagination started to reawaken and I came up with more interesting images and examples, played with the process more, and expanded on the characters, colors, situations, and ridiculousness of my images. As such, they became more memorable and formed more quickly.

It's true that, at first, it takes a minute or two to come up with a story for a new word, and when you multiply this by the many thousands of new words you may want to learn, it can seem terribly inefficient. But after doing this for a few days or a week, you get much better at it and can come up with a fantastic association in just a couple of seconds.

What about thinking through this silly story every time you want to recall a word? I've actually found that this approach acts more like glue, attaching the word to my memory, and it just becomes a natural part of my memory without me having to reapply the glue. Because of this, I generally only need to recall a story three or four times before I just *know* the word.

Now when I hear *gare* in French, I no longer need to go through the Garfield story. I just know this word means "train station." It's as much a part of me as its English equivalent. The way I got it into my memory is irrelevant; the point is that it's there now. For inspiration on keyword associations while you get better at creating your own, visit Memrise.com.

Spaced Repetition: Another Great Way to Build Vocabulary Quickly

If, however, the keyword method doesn't sound right for you, I've also had a lot of success using flash cards ordering the words or phrases by implementing what's known as the *spaced repetition* system.

Consider the way we traditionally learn vocabulary: We go through a list of new words in a book in the sequence in which they appear. Often we don't finish the list before we have to stop, and perhaps only halfway through that list. When we review the list the next time, we start again at the beginning. What's the problem with this? You never get to the end of the list. You just keep going over the words you already know, while you rarely reach the ones you don't know. You are effectively wasting your time on revising vocabulary that you already know well by now.

Spaced repetition uses flash cards and asks you to keep the hard words you didn't remember at the top of the deck and push to the bottom the words you already know. Essentially, the quicker you remember a word, the deeper in the deck it ends up. With physical flash cards, this is implemented by you. You make sure any "hard" words you didn't remember sit on the top of the deck and you slip the easy words much farther down in the stack. The quicker you remember a word, the farther down it should go.

My preference is to streamline this with technology using smartphone apps and free software, which let you order words based on their level of difficulty. By clicking a button, you can indicate how difficult that particular word is for you, and the app or software automatically reorders it. When I can, I spend a few days reviewing all my flash cards. This way I make sure important words are never forgotten, while I also come across new words.

Apps also allow you to study anywhere and at any time, even when you just have a few minutes while waiting for public transport or at any other time when you might be standing or sitting idly. Those little chunks of time throughout your day, which you are otherwise wasting, add up so quickly that you don't even need dedicated study time.

The app/program I prefer (which works on all systems) is called Anki. See download links for that app and some of my recommendations for other spaced-repetition tools at fi3m .com/srs.

Using Music to Learn Phrases

While learning words is certainly very important, I recommend you start with phrases or full sentences, which allow you to communicate real ideas from the start. Focusing on set phrases like "Where is the bathroom?" and "How much does that cost?" lets you communicate in grammatically correct forms without having to master grammar.

First, you need to know those phrases, though. Which isn't always easy.

To help retain a full sentence, I will often sing it out. This isn't something I necessarily came up with out of the blue. It's a technique used for centuries to remember passages. For instance, the Qur'an was originally taught orally, and people learned it by mimicking other people singing it. Even though it's in written form now, Muslims continue to sing many of its passages, which helps them remember and focus on important areas of it.

I combine singing with a little of the keyword method, so the start of a phrase gets my momentum going. Let's say I'm learning the Italian version of "Where is the bathroom?" which has one possible translation of "Dove si trova il gabinetto?"

The first part, *dove* (pronounced *doh-vay*), sounds a little like the word "duvet" (*doo-vay*). I imagine a duvet being used by a giant as toilet paper, or a toilet made out of bedcovers. The word itself actually means "where," so this isn't a useful keyword association, but I am only temporarily using it to get my phrase started. After you use a few phrases like this, you will start to just know that *dove* means "where" without requiring another mnemonic.

Next, let's think of a good tune to go with the phrase so we can sing it out—a short one, such as the famous Big Ben chime, will do the trick here. To remember I need to use this chime, I could visualize the Big Ben clock tower on its side (instead of standing upright), like a toilet paper roll holder. Remember, the more ridiculous your image, the easier it will be to recall.

To really get this going, I want you to sing this along with me. Come on! ♫ "Dove si trova . . . il gabinetto?" Can you hear it? Both of the two-syllable sets -*ve si* and -*etto* land on one note each, so the song fits with the phrase.

You don't have to actually sing it aloud every time you want to say the phrase; it's for mnemonic purposes only. And you only need to do it once or twice before you'll know the phrase naturally.

Memorizing Minute-Long Speeches for Smoother Intros

We've seen how to memorize single words and now phrases, so I want to end this chapter by going on to the next level and learning entire mini-scripts.

Mini-scripts are incredibly useful because we all tend to have similar conversations the first time we meet someone as beginning language learners: Who are you? Where are you from? What do you do for a living? Why are you learning this language? These phrases are used so frequently, in fact, you might as well just memorize the script so you can get through it more quickly and easily, as well as force yourself to move to the next stage in language learning.

The person you are speaking to will also be impressed that you can say these initial phrases so comfortably. Because of this, he or she is likely to use slightly more complex words with you, which will force you to keep up—an essential part of progressing through the different levels of fluency.

Another reason to do this is because recording a video in the language and then sharing it with your friends online can be excellent motivation and a great milestone to aim for in the early stages of your language learning project.

So I would highly recommend that you write out a script that would take perhaps one minute to recite, answering the four questions posed a few paragraphs ago, which you will likely need to answer when you first meet someone.

You can write out your script in English first, then talk to a native speaker (see the next chapter) to translate your answers for you precisely, so there are no mistakes (you should definitely not memorize phrases you get from computer-generated translations or any that you made yourself from piecing together dictionary translations), or you can use answers premade by native speakers that work for you, which you can find online or in a phrase book.

Now that you have your short script prepared, go ahead and start speaking it using a combination of everything you've seen in this chapter: create a flash card for each individual answer, then create a mnemonic for the first word or syllable of each phrase, and a chime pattern or song to go with that phrase, as we did previously.

Sometimes the story I have to tell about my travels and language learning can in itself be a minute-long answer. In this case, I sequence the story and attach each sequence to a mental image of something I can visualize as I'm speaking to that person. This can be a "memory palace" represented by a place you're familiar with, such as your childhood home or school, and you go through the most important rooms in a particular sequence and "peg" the relevant image in each room sequentially so you go through it in the right order.

Another thing I've done is use my own body as the cue for what I need to say. I might use the tip of my head to imagine a hat associated with the very first word, and then use my brain linked with the second item, my eyes with the third, my nose with the fourth, and so on, working my way down. For instance, when someone asked me why I was in Germany, I started with my backstory before telling that person about my improved language learning method and my plans for my stay in Berlin. So I started with a story about *school*, imagining a teacher whacking me across my head with electric eels, because the German word for "when" is *als*, which to my ears sounds close enough to "eels" for me to gain some confidence and momentum before I speak. "Als ich sechzehn Jahre alt war . . ." (When I was sixteen years old . . .) Now I knew where my story should begin (I was hit on the head, starting from the top of my body, where many short stories begin), the word to start the story with (*als*), and what I would actually talk about (when I was sixteen years old and finishing school, I got bad grades on my final German exam).

You obviously don't need to do this for all possible answers you could give. It's way too much work, and you should be forming your sentences naturally as soon as possible. But at the very beginning of this process, you are likely to repeat particular sentences, and it's perfectly fine—and perfectly efficient—to use tricks like this if they help you. Record a video of yourself going through the entire minute-long script of answers, without reading anything, and be ready to recite that script whenever asked by someone curious about why you are learning his or her language.

Starting a conversation off on the right foot can put you in a good mood and give you the momentum as a beginner to spontaneously produce other sentences much better. Learn what you need to say first and you will have that boost.

Words Are Your Arsenal

It is not important to be better than someone else,
but to be better than yesterday.

—Jigoro Kano, creator of judo

Each day, you can increase your vocabulary and thus your ability
to communicate ideas. Focus on learning new vocabulary,
phrases, and typical things you say often, and then burn them
into your memory so you can pull them out at a moment's notice.

Now try out some of the tools you've just learned:

• Pick one simple word in your target language that you don't
know yet and look it up or find it in a course book. Now think
about a hilarious or ridiculous way to associate a similar-
sounding English word with the translation of that word
using the examples listed in this chapter for inspiration. Then
do the same for other words. Test yourself on these words an
hour later, the next day, a week later, and you will see that
the keyword method makes them way more memorable.

• By the way, what's French for "train station"? What's the first
word in an Italian sentence asking where the bathroom is?
And how do you say "target" in Mandarin? As long as you
remembered even just one of these, you can start to see how
effective the keyword method is.

• If you are still stuck for ideas, check out Memrise.com for
some excellent mnemonics associated with common words in
many languages. Use this for inspiration to help you make up

your own associations for words you come across as you learn the language.

- Find translations of a handful of typical phrases like "What does that mean?" and use my music-association suggestion to help recall them.

- Write a short introduction to your personal story, answering the question "Why are you learning this language?" first in English. Make it short enough that you can provide the answer in about thirty seconds. Next, find a native speaker to help you translate it or proofread your own translation. Then use a combination of all the techniques mentioned in this chapter to help you go through the entire monologue without any help.

While these techniques are great for learning specific words and phrases, the best way to make sure you assimilate the natural use of a language is to actually use it. Familiarity is not built through flash cards and fun image associations, but through consistent use and seeing the words in context.

Use the tools in this chapter to help give yourself a boost with putting as many words as possible into your arsenal, but make sure you are also practicing as much as possible in real conversations so those words and phrases become a natural part of your language use. You will then learn even more words as you use the language.

For more on the concepts raised in this chapter, as well as videos, interviews, and relevant links, check out fi3m.com/ch–3.

CHAPTER 4

Immersion Without Buying a Plane Ticket

You don't need to be in a foreign country to learn the language. You can do it from the comfort of your home or local community.

You have likely realized by now what my "secret" is to learning languages. It has nothing to do with buying the right materials, finding the lazy or easy way to learn a language while you sleep or jog or participate in some other activity, or clicking your way through expensive language learning software.

You must *speak the language with other human beings*.

Soon enough, I will walk you through the process of how to keep a conversation flowing with a person, so we can start striving toward fluency, but first we have to actually find those people to speak with!

Many challenges may prevent you from speaking a language, but one I want to squelch right now is the idea that you can't speak a foreign language unless you're in that foreign country. This excuse has held too many people back for too long and we need to put a stop to it.

In this chapter, I delve into the many ways you can create an effective immersion environment and get genuine practice with native speakers of the language you are focused on without needing to buy a plane ticket. And I even suggest why it could be *better* to learn the language from home.

The Expat Problem

Visiting a country to learn its language isn't as great as you might think. When I first moved to Spain, I was under the delusion that something "in the air" would ensure that I simply picked up Spanish. I was in the country—what more could I possibly need?

Almost six months into my trip, I realized I needed much more. I could barely string together a few basic sentences. Sadly, my case is not the exception. In my travels, I have met literally thousands of expatriates, or expats, who barely speak the local language.

I met a man once in Prague who had lived there for a decade. He was married to a Czech woman and their children all spoke Czech. He told me that my understanding of the language after only two weeks was already way beyond his. I met people with similar stories in Poland, China, Thailand, France, and Germany. An entire *decade* in a country without speaking the language. I've met people all over the world who still don't know much of the local language beyond simple pleasantries, despite living there for several months or a year.

Of course, they all used many of the same excuses I outlined in chapter 1. But the real reason they didn't succeed was a combination of laziness and the temptations of what is called the *expat bubble,* both of which I succumbed to my first time in a non-English-speaking country.

The expat bubble is a protective shell of friendships that forms when a group of people live or work abroad for any length of time, and everyone within that bubble speaks your native language. When you arrive in a country, "just while you settle in," you go out with this group and speak English (or another language that isn't the local one). Sometimes working in your native language is unavoidable, but you still have many hours of free time that can be put to good use every day.

The problem is that the temptation to hang out with people you can relate to and express yourself with easily is so powerful that you end up making almost no local friends, or only meet local people who have excellent English language skills. This is exactly why people continue to think that "everyone speaks English."

Because so many people feel being in a country is the be-all and end-all solution to their problems, they start to believe that learning a new language is impossible when they don't speak it themselves after months of being exposed to it. So no, I do *not* think flying to a country is a crucial part of your language learning strategy.

On top of this, I have found that, with so many things to deal with when you move your entire life across the planet, all these distractions and mental strains wear you down. Even as an experienced language learner, I learned Mandarin more slowly than I might have because I had to deal with cultural integration issues as well as the language. It was a lot to take on at once.

Getting used to a new country, trying to make friends, dealing with loneliness, and facing the frustration of cultural differences are all distractions from learning the language. This is why I think it's actually better to learn a language in advance, before going to that country.

Spoken lessons via Skype are just as effective—and far more convenient. Instead of traveling to Taiwan, I would have been better off staying somewhere I was more familiar with, so the only project or challenge I had to think about was learning Mandarin.

Keep in mind this is coming from someone who has learned most of his languages by arriving in a country not speaking a word of the local language yet. There is indeed a certain sense of adventure and pressure to speak when you do this, but the other distractions can unfortunately take over and leave you unable to focus on the language. Is it any wonder so many people just give up and spend their entire time abroad with others from their own country?

When You Should Go to the Country

After hearing about all the distractions, you may think I'm about to tell you to avoid altogether the country that speaks your language and, instead, stay home forever. Quite the opposite. Being in a country and using its local language is such a wonderful experience, I cannot express it well enough in words.

Because I spoke the local language during my travels, I've listened as an old Czech lady told me about her experiences during World War II. I've eaten Easter dinner with four generations of Italians. I've appeared on TV and been interviewed on the radio in both Spanish and French long before I started my blog, talking about my experience as a foreigner. I've danced with a country's president. I've had an entire bar cheer me on as I sang karaoke in Tagalog in the Philippines. Honestly, I've had so many wonderful experiences that they could fill their own book, and my extensive travels mixed with cultural exploration has even led to me being awarded *National Geographic*'s title "Traveler of the Year"!

I am definitely not against the idea of moving to a country. As Saint Augustine famously said, "The world is a book, and those who do not travel read only one page."

But the thing is, I had all these wonderful experiences only when I was able to communicate well in the local language, not as I was learning the basics.

There is a lot of work at the beginning that is far less interesting than having "language adventures" with people, things like studying flash cards, repeating a basic phrase over and over again, or having the same introductory conversation about yourself repeatedly while you get comfortable using the language. You can get through it quickly, as I suggest in the next chapter, but you can't skip it. I say, do all this work from home so you can enjoy the much more fun part of language learning when you're in the country.

I think we should all strive to use the local language in a target country as soon as we can, even if our work or family responsibilities only allow us to take, say, a weeklong break to visit it. If you arrive already speaking the language well, you will have an absolutely wonderful week. And, of course, longer stays give you even more fantastic life experiences.

This is why I believe the most effective use of a plane ticket is to consider your looming departure date as motivation to work extra hard before you go, so you're able to maximize your experience in the country as soon as you step off the plane. Use an upcoming trip to motivate yourself to go through intensive speaking and study sessions in advance, so when you're there you don't have to do such activities and can focus on enjoying life through that language.

Attitude Versus Latitude

There are, however, many situations in which people successfully learn a language abroad. In many cases, they have done some advance work, but generally, when I hear about immersion courses, I find it's not being in the country that produces a successful language speaker, but that no one was allowed to speak English.

Because of this, immersion courses have started springing up in the wrong countries! There is an interesting concept in Spain: they create an "English village," they fly in English speakers, and

Spaniards from nearby towns or cities work on their English there—an English immersion experience that doesn't require a Spaniard to leave Spain. You can imagine how easy it would be to reverse this and have a "Spanish village" in English-speaking countries. Of course, we have these already in many multicultural neighborhoods.

This really shows that where you are isn't what decides whether or not you'll be successful. Attitude beats latitude (and longitude) every time. It's more about creating an immersion environment, exposing yourself to native speakers, and doing everything you can in that language.

The Human Factor

Exposure to human beings who speak your target language is what it's all about. If you can surround yourself with English speakers and maintain an English speaking bubble when in a foreign country, then surely the reverse is true, right? Why not surround yourself (physically or digitally) with native speakers of the language you are learning right from home?

It's time with real people and real exposure to the language through TV, radio, and movies that pushes you forward. And you can do this from anywhere.

I've been so adamant that time with human beings is the solution to any language learning problem that I've gone so far as to make a sales pitch for a Human Being product I call HB 2.0. Its features include:

- **Advanced voice-recognition and feedback-based correction:** Get instant corrections on your mistakes as you make them.

- **Context-based recognition:** Even if you do make mistakes, the system automatically adjusts for this and derives what you mean from the context. You are encouraged to attempt to do the same with the system yourself.

- **A completely natural language:** With an advanced memory bank of slang, idioms, and cultural references.

- **A pressure-based instant requirement to speak:** This feature is challenging, but it ensures you will improve on your level more quickly than you ever can in other learning systems.

- **An almost infinite database of interactive conversations:** You'll never run out of material to work on.

- **Built-in positive reinforcement:** This system automatically detects when you are running into difficulty and provides encouraging messages to get you back on track.

- **Complete portability:** You can access your HB 2.0 system on the go. Use it on buses, trains, while on walks, at social events, or from the comfort of your home.

Can you see how I've phrased these as if I were pitching some language learning software? We keep trying to find language learning solutions through courses, software, apps, flights abroad, books, schools, and a host of other methods, some of which can be useful, but these are nothing but accessories to the true core of language learning: the people we speak with and hear.

Couch-Surfing for Language Practice

The trick, then, is finding native speakers who will give you that wonderful language practice. A great way to do this is through websites.

The website I have gotten the most use out of by far is Couchsurfing.org. This site is well known among budget travelers as a means to connect with people living in cities around the world who invite you to sleep on their couches (couch-surf). I haven't used this aspect of the site much myself, even though I travel a lot and was among the first ten thousand members to sign up. The reason I use it is because it's one of the largest social networking sites and it lets you search through its members by language. All you need to do is search for the city you live in and limit the criteria to profiles listing the language you are learning (or maintaining).

I've used Couchsurfing.org to practice Italian in Amsterdam, Esperanto in Colombia, American Sign Language in Hong Kong, Dutch in Istanbul, and many other unlikely combinations, all by messaging whoever spoke a particular language and inviting that person out for coffee or lunch.

The great thing about the site is that the nature of its members, being world travelers, means they are quite open-minded and much more likely to meet up with an interesting new stranger than other communities might.

Then again, you can use the site for the purpose it was designed for and host people traveling through your town. This way everyone wins: the travelers get free accommodation and you get to practice a language. Over the span of a few years I've hosted almost two thousand people. Each profile has references, so you know you can trust the person, and nothing in my house has ever gone mysteriously missing. Plus, I have had only positive experiences due to being selective about whom I choose to host.

As well as inviting people to coffee or lunch and hosting people, I have gone to Couchsurfing.org's many meet-ups, where I always find an international crowd, many of whom speak the language I want to practice. In international cities, there are even meet-ups and parties specifically for practicing particular languages.

Other Social Searches

Similarly, InterNations.org hosts social events in major cities, which draw a very good mixture of people from many different countries. You can see in advance which nationalities will be attending, with a per-country count in the meet-up summary, to be sure you have a good chance of meeting someone to practice your target language with.

Another great site is Meetup.com, which may not have as international a crowd, but does have specific meet-ups aimed at practicing particular languages. Other sites are suggested in the online chapter summary page.

Of course, each of these sites is much more potent when used in an international city that is likely to have visitors, but I've been surprised at finding unlikely languages even in small towns.

Keep in mind that even if you don't find a premade meet-up on Meetup.com or Couchsurfing.org for the language you want to practice, you can create one yourself. At first, just a couple of people may show up, but it could grow and become a regular event for those who want to speak some Spanish or Mandarin or Japanese.

Any social networking site may have a way to set up language meet-ups. Even Facebook has groups for particular cities (search "[your city name] + [language name]" to see if you can find one), and if it doesn't, set one up yourself to connect with other learners. If you don't find native speakers, working with other learners can be beneficial too.

In the past I even went so far as to use dating sites to get language practice, although this is obviously one approach you want to use carefully. These sites also let you search its users by language.

In-Person Opportunities

I do a lot of stuff online, but there are plenty of offline alternatives that can help you get in touch with people for language practice.

For instance, if you live near a university, you will certainly find an advertisement board where you can leave your request for a "language exchange." Many universities have exchange students from abroad who are learning your native language and are eager to practice.

Even if they don't speak the language you want, ask your friends and family for advice to see if they know communities you could join to practice your language in person. Sometimes groups meet up at a local library, or notices in local newspapers advertise such meet-ups. Just ask around, and you'll be surprised what you find.

Social Skydiving

Life begins where your comfort zone ends.

Another option for the more adventurous among us is to simply walk up to someone you don't know who is using your target language, or otherwise appears to be from that country, and strike up a conversation. Many cities have large communities of foreigners who are pleasantly surprised when a local person tries to speak to them in their own language.

An excellent example of someone who takes advantage of this adventurous approach is Moses McCormick (whom I mentioned in the introduction), who lives in Columbus, Ohio. Columbus isn't a city you would immediately think of as international, but Moses shows us how much practice you can get in many languages anywhere in the world.

Moses and I went together to a shopping mall, and he showed me how easy it was. He stopped strangers and asked nonintimidating questions to break the ice, such as asking what time it was or whether that person knew where the mall arcades were. When they replied, he continued by casually asking where they were from. If they were from a country whose language he knew, he would then ask, in their language, whether they spoke that language. Simple as that. We did it for a couple of hours and found that each interaction was pretty positive—some people were busy working, so they could only speak for a moment, but nobody was angered or frustrated by our attempts. We recorded the experience, so you can watch it on YouTube and see how it went.

This is good for some quick practice, but you can also ask people if they'd like to meet up later to chat some more in their language. Believe it or not, people are nice, even with strangers, and the many excuses you might come up with about making someone angry by such interactions are usually just in your head.

I try to be friendly when I first meet people, and those meetings have pretty much always worked out well. When you are genuine and truly passionate about learning a language, people can tell. They are often open to a quick chat, even when they have just met you.

Hopefully this shows you that there are many in-person opportunities to practice with others who speak the language you are interested in. As long as you live in a sizable city and are learning a pretty widely spoken language, you will surely find those opportunities if you look hard enough. Don't give up after the first attempt. Some smaller towns or less common languages may make this trickier, but there may still be someone out there, ready to share a conversation.

Learning with Other Non-Natives

When looking to practice your target language, you may think learning can only occur when you speak with a native speaker of that language. Try to focus on finding these natives, using the suggestions in this chapter. The further you get in your language learning attempts, the more essential it is to get genuine native exposure.

However, if you are a beginner and finding it hard to get practice time with native speakers, never forget that other learners like you are also excellent for practice. Because you are both learners, there is less of a feeling of embarrassment when you make mistakes, and you can relate to each other's mistakes. You won't necessarily learn from or correct your mistakes as efficiently when practicing with another learner, but the confidence to simply use a language is just as essential as vocabulary and grammar, and all practice helps you gain confidence.

It's also great to bounce those learned phrases off someone else and have that person challenge you by asking follow-up questions (even if his or her grammar isn't perfect), so you can work out what to say and know which words you need to learn before the questions come up again.

You can arrange to sit down with a friend and regularly practice a language. Once you are used to speaking the language at a basic level, you'll be more confident to try a conversation with a native speaker when the opportunity comes.

Consuming Media at a Distance

As well as spending time with natives, a priority for our spoken focus, you should also work to improve your reading and listening comprehension skills. To do this, you need "virtual immersion" by surrounding yourself with the language.

The first thing to do is find streamed radio broadcasts from the country where your target language is dominant. Next, you can find dubbed versions of your favorite TV shows in the language you're trying to learn. Find out what the series is called in that language by looking up its English title on Wikipedia and seeing the translation referred to in the column along the left side of the show's page. Then search Amazon.com or another online store for that foreign title and buy the DVD or download it. In some cases, depending on the language, you can even buy an international DVD in your favorite local or online store that includes dubbing in the language you are interested in, or download the video with alternative language selection options.

You can do the same for foreign-language editions of your favorite movies, books, and comics. Or, instead of relying on dubbed or foreign-language versions of the items and programs you are familiar with, check out that country's favorite shows or movies. Ask a language partner or teacher for advice on what to watch, and see if you can access it from where you live.

Other than this, there are numerous online sources that give you content in other languages. You can find an updated list of some great examples at fi3m.com/langs.

Online Language Exchange

What we've talked about so far applies to in-person meetings and media, but there is a whole new world of opportunities awaiting you!

A few decades ago you would have been right in saying that getting spoken-language practice while living in more remote areas, or with a less common language, was too hard to accomplish. But today we have a wonderful resource connecting us with native speakers just about anywhere—the Internet. With this, there is really no excuse for not finding opportunities to practice your target language.

For those of us who speak English as a native language, there are countless people from other countries eager to get some English practice. If you provide them with thirty minutes of your time to chat in English and answer some of their questions, then they will teach you their language free of charge.

This language-exchange idea is popular, especially online. English and other languages are in high demand, so you can find an exchange much more easily than you think.

My favorite way to do language exchanges is on a site dedicated to that purpose, such as Italki. You can search for language partners, arrange a time in advance, and see references from others who have spoken to a particular person before, so you know whether this person is more likely to be helpful and friendly. Connect to my profile by signing up via fi3m.com/italki.

Other places to find language partners include forums, such as the free one on my site (fi3m.com/forum), where people post their languages offered and anyone interested can get in touch for your Skype details. Alternative sites to search for language partners are mentioned in chapter 10. There are many options, so with a little searching you will indeed find speaking opportunities that could theoretically keep you busy many hours each day using your target language.

You can also arrange for paid lessons online. While one-on-one lessons may seem beyond your budget, when you are interacting with people in countries where you can leverage currency differences, you can get excellent lessons for a good price. An hour of Chinese lessons from a good teacher who doesn't live in a major city, such as Beijing or Shanghai, can be easily found for five dollars or so an hour on Italki. The same goes for French teachers based in Africa, Spanish teachers in South America, and so on.

Thanks to the wonderful opportunities on the web, I was able to learn the majority of my Egyptian Arabic *entirely online* while staying in Belo Horizonte, deep within Brazil. In this city, I couldn't find a single speaker of the dialect I was focused on, but I still managed to speak it for several hours each day, thanks to my online teachers. After three months of speaking exclusively via Skype, I was ready to go to Egypt and travel using conversational Arabic, which helped me appreciate my time there much more than if I had arrived just to study or knowing next to nothing of the language. When preparing this book, I learned Japanese while living in Valencia, Spain, similarly practicing for hours each day via Skype.

Now that you know how to find native speakers and remember words and phrases, it's time to actually *speak* your target language.

A Stranger Is Just a Friend You Haven't Met Yet

There are no strangers here, only friends you haven't yet met.

—W. B. YEATS

I always keep this Irish saying in mind when I'm out and about and notice someone who seems worth talking to or an interesting language learning opportunity appears. This can also be applied to all the "strangers" you can connect with online.

There are so many ways to practice your target language without traveling abroad. Here is a recap of ideas:

- Check out Couchsurfing.org, InterNations.org, Meetup.com, or the groups on any of the social networking sites like Facebook and Google+. You're bound to connect with people who speak the language you wish to practice.

- Do a search on Italki.com (sign up at fi3m.com/italki first) for a language partner who wants to learn your target language, or find an affordable private teacher. In both cases, practice the language using Skype.

- To see the video of Moses and me speaking multiple languages in a mall in Columbus, Ohio, or to check out Moses's videos demonstrating how he frequently does this, go to fi3m.com/moses.

For up-to-date website suggestions, encouragement for approaching people, videos, and other links relevant to this chapter, see fi3m.com/ch–4.

CHAPTER 5

Speaking from Day One

> Start speaking a new language
> right away with easy-to-follow "cheats" for when
> you don't know the words you want to say.

We have finally arrived at the most important advice I give anyone who is serious about learning to speak a language: you have to speak it from day one.

Studying for eons until some vague "I'm ready" day is not the way to go about it. Speaking the language out loud with a real human being, whether in person or online, *every single day* is the best way by far to zoom forward toward a conversational language level and onward to fluency.

If you really think about it, what's the biggest mistake you can possibly make with a language? Using the wrong word? Making a grammatical error? No. The biggest mistake is not getting your message across. Since the goal of a language is communication, your top priority should not be to sound perfect, but to make yourself understood. Even if you know only a couple of words, you will be far more effective using those few words than you ever will be remaining silent.

This advice to start speaking the language *right now* prompts many language learners to list all the reasons why it is not possible to do so, but I hope this chapter convinces you that it's not only possible, it's so easy you'd have to be crazy *not* to give it a try.

How to Speak When You Don't Have the Words Yet

The first thing someone might say when I suggest speaking from day one is "I haven't learned any words yet!" How can you speak when you are starting with absolutely nothing? Surely you should study for a while first and *then* speak when you're "ready."

Well, there's no such thing as "ready" in language learning. There will simply never be a day when you are 100 percent ready. You just have to use whatever you know, even if you have only been studying for a few hours.

You are not actually starting a new language from absolutely nothing. As explained in chapter 6, there are always cognates and common words you have when you start off. And we each have decades of experience with context, body language, and other social cues.

Speaking during the first hours of your very first one-on-one conversation is not about spitting out thousands of words, but about knowing just enough words to ask and answer a couple of questions, hearing the first instances of the language used naturally, and challenging yourself to try to understand a little bit more the next time. You learn by *doing*—by trying to speak, making mistakes, and learning from them so the next time you make fewer mistakes.

You always have enough words for some level of communication with people. The trick is being okay with the fact that you can't have any deep conversations just yet and working through the simpler conversations first, so you can get to those more interesting chats sooner.

The First Hours

What exactly will you do during those first hours? Keep in mind that you are going to have only a basic question-and-answer first exchange with someone.

Make a Plan for Your First Conversation

- Decide that you will walk up to someone you have heard speaking your target language or you know would be a good partner for language practice, or

- e-mail someone through a social networking site and set a specific time for a coffee meet-up, or

- set up a language exchange online via Skype.

Now that you have scheduled your first conversation, you have a deadline in place to work toward. This makes it much more real than learning random words and grammar rules that you may need "someday."

Spend a Couple of Hours Preparing

- You can find a pretty good selection of premade phrases in travel phrase books. These books also come with a pronunciation guide, so you don't have to worry about the phonetics of the language yet.

- Learn some phrases through free online courses or free phrase or language books from your local library.
  Phrases to start with:

  "How are you?"

  "What's your name?"

  "My name is . . ."

  "I don't understand."

  "Could you repeat that?" (Or the shorter *"Again, please."*)

  "Can you speak slower please?"

  "What does [fill in the blank] mean?" (Or *"What does that mean?"*)

- Use the keyword method for individual words or set phrases like "Yes," "No," "Please," "Thank you," "Hello," and "Good-bye," although it's very likely you know some, if not all of these already!

This isn't such a huge demand on your first day of learning a language. No conjugation tables, no lists of the top thousand most frequently used words, no memorizing every possible sequence of sentences—just a few phrases and words for a very limited first exchange. Even if you claim to be a terrible language learner, you can manage this, especially if you apply some of my memorization suggestions or an alternative you prefer.

Your First Conversation

The time comes and you have an opportunity to speak in the mother tongue of your conversation partner for the first time! The curtains open, the spotlight focuses on you, and all you have to do is say . . . "Hello."

The person replies with "Hello." You return a "How are you?" which may be followed by "Fine, and you?" Just take it one phrase at a time.

Perhaps you are able to follow three or four entire question-and-answer exchanges based on the phrases you think are likely to come up, or maybe it's just two exchanges before the person says something you don't understand. This is not the point when you give up, but the point when you say, "I don't understand. Could you repeat that?" See if you can extrapolate from what is said next.

Rather than feel like you failed if you have to stop at some point, think of these early exchanges as your first successful conversations in a foreign language. Maybe the exchange lasts twenty seconds, or maybe just ten. The point is that you are at a very different stage now compared to where you were before this conversation.

Appreciate this moment, even if you have to switch to English or another language.

Cheating When You Don't Know a Word

Okay, so you've survived the first few moments of your first conversation. After that, even if the exchanges last no more than ten seconds before you decide to switch to English or say good-bye to the native speaker, you can go back to your books or notes and refresh your memory with what you *thought* you knew or wanted to say but couldn't remember. Add these phrases to a flash card deck and make sure to study them.

From here, you simply repeat the process and learn more phrases and words. You will find you can expand those ten seconds to twenty or thirty, and eventually to an entire minute.

Early conversations may always be the same. Give yourself a little momentum. In fact, try to learn the first ten seconds—both your side and a few likely replies—by heart, because starting off well is essential, and this part of any first conversation is incredibly predictable.

Generally, during my first conversations, I find I cannot cram for all the possible words and phrases I might want to say. It's just too much to process in too little time, no matter how good my memory techniques are, especially since the techniques are better suited to long-term recall rather than short-term cramming. Because of this, I "cheat" a little and carry some notes with me.

If I am Skyping someone for my first conversation, I'll leave open a text file with a list of things I want to say and some tough words I haven't learned well enough yet, like "engineer" and "writer." If I am sitting with someone in a café, say, I'll have a little sheet of notes I can glance at for reference. This person will already be well aware that I'm a beginning learner so he or she won't be surprised or offended when I'm in need of "training wheels."

My notes will also include some words that might come up on the spot, or I might bring along my phrase book and use the dictionary in the back to quickly look something up. If I'm on a computer using Skype, I'll use Google Translate or an online dictionary specific to that language. This way I'm not limited by my active memory, which at the very start of this process may have a couple dozen words ready at best.

Keep It Simple, Stupid: Rephrasing to Keep the Flow

One thing you will quickly learn at this beginner stage is to phrase what you want to say in your mother tongue before you "translate" it into the target language. Translating as a long-term strategy is a bad idea if you want real fluency, as this extra step will slow you down too much. But you will be speaking slowly as a beginner, so it's okay to think of what you want to say in English first and then translate it.

Let's say, for instance, that the conversation veers toward your future plans, and initially you decide you want to say, "I will travel to Spain in July for a two-week vacation." But then you realize you don't know how to use the future tense ("will") confidently enough yet, you have forgotten the verb for "to travel," and you can't even remember the words for "July" or "vacation."

A traditional language learner would probably give up at this point, resigned that he or she is not "ready" yet, and switch to English or avoid the topic entirely. But someone focused on *communication,* rather than saying precisely the right thing, will look at ways to rephrase with different words so what is used effectively conveys the same meaning.

Rather than worry about future verb-tense conjugations, many languages have a handy feature of sticking to infinitive verb forms after modal verbs. In less complex language, this means that if you use words like "want," "need," "would like," "should," "may," "can (able to)" in their standard present-tense conjugation with, say, "I" ("I want," "I can"), you can follow them up with the dictionary (infinitive) form of the important verb you wish to use, such as "to travel." When you think of it, the essential difference between "I want to travel" and "I will travel," while important, is not significant when you want to convey a simple meaning.

To keep it simple, I'd recommend you learn just "I want," "you want," "I can," and "you can" to begin with, especially if your exchanges are directly with one person (since the he/she/it/they pronouns will be less relevant in that situation). The word "want" can be an okay replacement for the future tense ("want to speak" instead of "will speak"). "Can" is good to use in many direct questions, so rather than "Do you speak Italian?" I would go for "Can you speak Italian?" The point of doing this is to use the standard dictionary form of the word "speak" (*parlare* in Italian) without needing to conjugate (change) it. "Need" (or "have to") is good for any kind of obligation. So rather than "I start work at nine," I might say, "I need to start work at nine." The meaning isn't precisely the same but it's close enough.

This isn't pharmaceutical science or bridge-building engineering, where a tiny mistake could cost lives. This method will be used in a casual first conversation with a native speaker who is aware of the fact you are still learning. Always go for "close enough" and search your mind for words that have similar meanings, even if they aren't necessarily synonymous.

So moving on with my original example phrase, the next word I wanted to say was "travel," but it's still day one or two and I may not know this word yet. Although, I have learned "to go," so I can use that instead! "To go to Spain" and "to travel to Spain" are essentially the same thing.

In terms of having more conversations earlier in your learning process, simple all-encompassing verbs and adjectives will get you much further than a wide scope of vocabulary will. So "very good" for a beginner is a fine alternative in most contexts to "wonderful," "delicious," "nice," "great," "admirable," "talented," "friendly," and so many other words. It isn't a great alternative, but it will do. Later you can convey your thoughts precisely, but for now focus on saying something. Besides, saying that a meal is "very good" is

infinitely better than absolutely needing to use the word "delicious"
but not remembering it and instead saying nothing.

Whenever I can't remember a word I want, I pause and quickly try to think of alternatives. What's another way to say it in English, and, most important, do I know that word in this language yet?

With that in mind, "to go" will do fine for "to travel" for beginners.

With "July," try to think of anything vaguely similar. Let's say you happen to know the word for "summer." It doesn't mean the same thing as "July," but it's close enough. If not, you could also say "in two months" or "soon" or "later" or "when I can" or a host of other alternatives that convey your general meaning while also keeping the conversation flowing.

For "vacation," I could say that I want "to be a tourist." This isn't quite something I would say in English regularly, but the meaning is clear enough, and the word for "tourist" is similar in many languages.

So we have just turned "I will travel to Spain in July for a two-week vacation" into "I want to go to Spain this summer to be a tourist for two weeks." There is essentially no difference in these two phrases, except that the second may be much easier for you to say if you already know these words in your target language.

Keep it simple, as I said, and always remember that you can convey the meaning of what you want to say as long as you are flexible about *how* you say it. Not using precisely the right words is a temporary sacrifice so that you can find your flow in the language and reach an intermediate stage much faster. Then you will be able to start using those more precise words. Go through this slightly frustrating stage of using simpler words for a short time, and you will sound much more articulate sooner!

The First Days

This doesn't mean that you will only talk about something as mundane as the weather during these first exchanges. I personally don't care much for discussing the weather, in any language, including English. For me, it's more interesting to find out what the person did that day or if that person has plans, and then to talk about my plans for the day. At this stage, a phrase book starts to become less helpful, even though it still has plenty of useful nuggets.

Speaking incorrectly is fine. I may say something like "This morning I wake up at eight A.M." (rather than "*woke* up") or go full-out Tarzan mode and say "Tomorrow dance." You will start to feel minor successes when you get a look or reply that implies you were understood.

If you are in a more formal learning environment, such as a language exchange or an affordable private lesson, then your teacher might correct you. Make a note of it so you get it right the next time. And this is the trick: feedback is essential when you start inventing your own phrases.

Continue to expand your conversation skills, repeating things you said in a previous spoken session, but this time saying them a little bit more confidently. If you find that particular phrases come up often, script out a predictable exchange and memorize it. This way you can get that entire first minute down, and then move on to the second minute.

When new material comes up, add it to the script. Relying on predictable patterns is not a good long-term strategy at all, but remember, you need to change your strategy as you progress in a language. Most things I discuss in this chapter are not applicable to anyone working on moving from conversational level to fluency, and later toward getting confused for a native speaker, which I discuss in later chapters.

What will happen in these first days, though, is that you'll get so used to saying particular phrases, they start to seem natural, and you can experiment with using new words and combining them with your previous sentences, replacing other, simpler words.

When you are talking with someone who is there specifically to help you improve your language skills, that person will be more than patient and will work with you on these basic conversations, adding a little more to what you can do each day and hopefully challenging you with new words and new concepts. Build on what you are confident about—through both actual practice and solid memorization between spoken sessions—and add to that over time. This way you'll start to get a foundation in the language.

Apply a Triage System to What You Learn

Constant conversation practice is the core of what I would recommend to people with a spoken-communication focus in their language, as opposed to those who are learning a language to pass an exam or to read it well. All of your study attempts should be about making that *next* spoken session a little bit better.

This gives you a more immediate experience, and you can work on your language skills more directly. This is vastly superior to taking generic courses that try to prepare you to speak a language fluently "someday" instead of right away. Despite this, I recommend sometimes returning to a traditional language course, especially if you find one more appropriate to your needs than those with a spoken focus (such as Teach Yourself, Colloquial, and Assimil courses), and go through the course recommendations alone or with a teacher, as long as you solve your biggest spoken issues first. This way you are working on your day-to-day issues in tandem with the more general issues and topics you need to cover in this language.

When you come to an aspect in your course that you don't feel is super relevant to you right now, skip it. This might be, say, a grammar feature you don't see as fitting your "triage" system. Good courses tend to have relevant information pop up at the right times, but when a course is very tourist focused, it may include something like how to ask for directions, which would not be a priority for you if you're preparing for a Skype lesson and would prefer to ask your conversation partner what he or she did that day.

Concentrating on a triage system of learning requires a much more active effort on the part of the learner. Take an active role in your language learning story and you'll go much further.

But I Can't Understand the Reply!

Up to now, I've been focusing on what you want to say. There is another person in the equation, however, and that person may not come up with the replies you were expecting—and therefore the dialogue you have studied.

Most things you will hear at the start of your language learning adventure will seem incomprehensible. It is essential to accept this and not be so surprised by it. Other people will be hard to understand—especially at first. Audio lessons associated with courses tend to be recorded in soundproof rooms with people speaking unnaturally slowly and clearly. Audio files that you can pause and replay are quite different from what someone less experienced teaching foreigners might say, even if that person is technically saying the same phrase.

This is why I don't try to understand an entire phrase in the early stages.

Listen for any particular words or segments of a person's speech that you *can* understand, and extrapolate what is being said from that. We do this all the time, even in our native languages. If I were to talk to you over a bad telephone connection and you heard me say " . . . dinner . . . six P.M. . . . think?" with everything else drowned out by noise or static, it would be reasonable for you to extrapolate that I'm inviting you out for dinner and I perhaps ended with "What do you think?"

I consider my progress in language learning comprehension to be nothing but a constant attempt to improve the quality of this telephone call. It's very fuzzy at first and gets clearer with time. I may start with only understanding one word out of every one hundred, but after a few days, I pick up two or three more words, then ten, and so on.

So rather than thinking I *don't understand,* imagining that what you just heard could be anything, realize that it *can't* be anything; it has to be related to what you were just talking about, within reason. What is this person likely to be saying in this context, which single word or words did you understand, and based on that, what can you imagine with reasonable confidence was said back to you?

My Two-Hour Polish Experience

When I visited Poland to speak at a conference, I was too preoccupied with my TEDx presentation (in English) to spend time learning the language over the long term as I usually tend to do. I did, however, manage to invest two hours in learning a little of the language, and I was able to use my Polish after such a very short learning period despite its notoriety for being among the hardest languages to learn.

You can learn from my experience. Here's a step-by-step guide to your own first Skype language session, if you want to give it a try:

- Use a phrase book to learn some basic phrases related to your anticipated first conversation, and prepare other phrases using a dictionary. For example:

  "I just started learning Polish."
  "I am going to Poland soon."

- Since you'll be using a computer, look up online words in the dictionary that you think will come up in the conversation with your teacher, knowing that they will be encouraging you to do most of the talking.

- Open a text document onscreen to use as a "cheat" for words you aren't confident you will remember. Have several dozen prepared.

- Whenever your teacher says a word you don't know, ask him or her to type it in the chat window, then copy it and paste it into Google Translate or a better language-specific dictionary (for a list of completely free online dictionaries by language, please see fi3m.com/dict).

When I connected with my teacher via Skype, thanks to my prepared phrases, I managed to keep my side of the conversation going for half an hour. Only Polish came out of my mouth, but of course I was "cheating" with my prepared vocabulary list.

During this half hour, there were many times when I didn't understand, and I admitted that. There were times when I wanted to say something very simple but didn't have the words or couldn't look up the words quickly enough, so I had to try to change the subject. It was far from perfect, but as I keep saying, it will always be far from perfect, just less so with time.

Next, I had another half hour to improve on what I had done during the first conversation plus prepare specific questions for a friend, Goshka, whom I was meeting in a mall.

I wanted to record this first-ever in-person interaction in Polish on camera, so the first question I asked her when we met was "Is it okay if I record this conversation?" Of course I couldn't find this phrase in my dictionary, so I just went with "Problem with camera?" and pointed at it, fully aware that my grammar was way off. But she understood me and said, "No."

I went on to ask her what she was doing today, even though I already knew what she was doing—I had already invited her out for a coffee and to meet up with some readers of my blog. So when she said that, I can only confidently say that I understood "coffee," "blog," and "Benny" (as in Benny's blog), but based on those words coming up and the question I had asked, I understood what the entire phrase was likely to have been.*

Whenever I didn't understand what she or any other Polish speaker said, I smiled and laughed a little at my own silliness to help the other person feel more at ease, rather than switch to another language. It worked. The conversations stayed entirely

---

* You can see a segment of my Polish Skype conversation and my video with Goshka—both with subtitles—at fi3m.com/polish-in-1-hour.

in Polish in both my Skype exchange and my time with Goshka, minus the rare clarifications, even though I had just started to learn the language.

As I progress in a language and understand more of what is being said to me, I have to rely less and less on extrapolation and what I call *contextese*. I'll never stop using these entirely, but I will eventually rely on them almost as infrequently as I do in English.

I have a strange suggestion for you: spend two weeks learning Esperanto. A study in Sweden found that students who had been learning French for two years were outperformed by those who had learned Esperanto for one year and then French for just one year. They had ultimately learned less French but actually did better in French exams!

You don't need a whole year, though; keep in mind that you are not in an academic environment, using traditional study methods and only for a couple of hours each week. I find that with an efficient learning approach and working at it intensively for just two weeks (or longer, if you can't do it so intensively), you can make a lot of progress in a language. The reason I'm suggesting Esperanto is that it was intentionally designed to be the easiest language you could possibly learn. It was artificially created in the nineteenth century and has gained a lot of support with a very strong community behind it. As such, you can easily find someone willing to have a practice chat with you in Esperanto!

One of the best resources for this I've found is Lernu.net. The forums and chat rooms will have other people to practice with, and the site has a detailed (and completely free) course to teach you the language. Because it's so straightforward, you won't have much grammar to drag you down, and the vocabulary is very easy to learn.

Since Esperanto is so easy, you can get much further in it in a very short period and focus on using the language, rather than studying complex grammar or vocabulary tables. This means you can conquer that hard aspect of language learning: simply getting used to communicating in a language that isn't your own. This shift in mentality can be applied to your next language, and I have found that you can potentially shave months off your learning period for any other language with just this two-week investment. Thanks to Esperanto, you can remove this setback of not being confident about using any foreign language.

Also, the Esperanto community is incredibly welcoming, friendly, and provides one of the best introductions you could have to the language learning world. I have many lifelong friends thanks to this language! For much more information about Esperanto, including videos of me speaking it, please check out fi3m.com/esperanto.

Keep It All in That Language ASAP

Your conversations in the target language, even at the very start, must be just in that language. No English! This is the core of a truly communicative learning approach.

A traditional academic way to learn a language, on the other hand, teaches you how the language works in your mother tongue. Your teacher essentially speaks in the wrong language—English—for the entire session as you dissect the target language's grammar and vocabulary, just as you might a frog in a biology class.

Don't treat your language like a collection of facts you have to learn, as if it were a history or mathematics lesson or a set of rules to follow. You can't learn a language efficiently this way. Language is a means to communicate and should be learned and used as such from the start.

That's precisely why I promote a speak-from-day-one approach. You genuinely speak in that language and hear that language spoken back to you from day one. This means that you must eliminate, or at least drastically reduce, any other language use during the time you are focused on your target language.

Everything coming out of your mouth should be in the right language.

While I was able to do this with Polish, when I started learning Arabic, it took me about two weeks to keep my side of the conversation all in Arabic. I did use some Arabic in my first lesson, but I kept switching back to English. It wasn't because Arabic was more difficult for me; it was that I doubted myself and lacked the courage to take the leap.

When I finally did, I realized that I could have done this much earlier, and should have, to force myself to progress quickly. But it's hard. It's embarrassing, frustrating, annoying, and exhausting. (In my earlier learning stages, I felt like my brain was melting after a good spoken session.)

You must pass through this if you want to get to the more fun bit. Keeping your sessions mostly in the wrong language will do nothing but slow your progress. This is why it can take years to learn a language; if you spend years not actually using it, of course, you can't have even the simplest of conversations.

Once you make the decision to keep your conversation in the *right* language—your target language—do not under any circumstances allow yourself to break from that resolution. Look up a word if you don't know it, or use simple language work-arounds with words you *do* know. You may think that saying the precise word you want to use in English instead of the target language helps the conversation, but it hinders your language learning progress.

The trick is to make this decision as soon as possible. You can do it on day one, as long as you are okay with long pauses while you look up words (and you can tell your teacher or other speaker that he or she should translate or spell words for you to look up, to help you with understanding them), but it's very frustrating. This is all about mind over matter and just accepting the frustration. Once you do, you can get through it much faster.

What If the Person Replies in English?

When I'm an absolute beginner with a language, I still prefer a person to reply to me in the language I'm learning, but I may sometimes allow that person to say words in English because even if the person tried to explain them to me in my target language, it may be beyond my capabilities to understand the explanation. Individual words in English are okay, or a sentence, if necessary, but most of the time you should be hearing just the target language. You need to get used to thinking in that language, and relying on translations the entire time is not useful for this.

If you are paying for a teacher, explain very clearly and sternly that you are paying that person to speak your target language, not your native language. The teacher has to work to maintain the right language and be imaginative with how it's done. If I say this to a teacher and the person keeps switching back to English for too long, I am wasting my money and don't request any further lessons. Because of this, when I start to learn a language, I may go through several teachers, eliminating the "worst" based mostly on their inability to help me progress using just (or at least 99 percent of the time) that language. For me, the mark of a good teacher is how imaginative he or she is while making sure that English is only ever used as a last resort.

If you are in a language exchange, the same rules apply. You are helping someone during the twenty- or thirty-minute segment of the exchange that is in your language. That time is for the other person to learn. But when it's your turn, he or she needs to be patient and helpful with you and not make the switch. If the person doesn't try hard enough, then once again consider whether or not this is the best person to do an exchange with you.

There are plenty of paid teachers and language exchanges online, so you are well within your rights to shop around until you find someone you can genuinely learn with. When you give something in exchange (money or your teaching), this person is wasting your time by not keeping in the right language.

Let's say you meet someone who speaks your target language, and you ask this person in that language "How are you?" or say some other phrase to start a conversation, but the person replies in English. Don't lose hope. In my experience, this is not meant as an insult regarding your level in the language or a refusal to help you. The person may instead not be aware how serious you are about practicing. If you say (again, in that language) how very interested you are in learning this beautiful language and how much you would really appreciate any help, even with just a couple of minutes' practice, most of the time you'll find this person appreciates your passion and will stay in the right language.

It's a lot to ask of a stranger, to listen to an absolute beginner for a very long period, so just request two to five minutes for some quick practice, in a case like this. Unless this person is busy, it's hardly a major inconvenience, and in most cultures and for most people, I have found them to be overjoyed by a learner's enthusiasm and willing to stick to the right language. They may even offer to meet up with you later or gladly keep helping you for much longer than a couple of minutes.

If you face any reluctance, offer something in exchange. Rather than payment, though, you can make the conversation interesting for them in many other ways:

- I travel a lot, and in my initial years, people would ask me how on earth I managed to travel so much without being super rich. What I had to say was something they were very interested in hearing. Because of this, I found that they listened attentively and helped me enthusiastically with their language. They were interested in my explanations of how I found cheaper flights, haggled apartment prices down, and discovered other ways to afford my travels—and this was despite being at a beginning or slow conversation level and making lots of mistakes.

- Explain the many ways that non-English speakers can get free English practice, such as where they can find a local expat community or the best websites for meeting up with English speakers to get online practice, and give them other language learning tips . . . but do it all in their language. This way you can feel that you've been way more helpful in return, more than giving them just a few minutes of English practice, and can get them in touch with those who would be very happy to speak English with them, if you would personally prefer not to.

- Finally, if someone insists on using English with you, and you are in that person's country, it's important to point out that you are the one who has moved across the planet to learn a new language, so it's unfair of this person to insist on speaking English. If nothing is coming out of the conversation, you may have to simply move on to someone else.

When I made the tough decision to change my entire life routine (at the time) and speak only Spanish, I discovered to my disappointment that many Spaniards were only hanging out with me to get free English practice. I lost several friends when I stuck to my guns about this decision, but I also made many *new* friends, not just in Spain but elsewhere over the many years since I've been able to speak Spanish. I'm very glad I didn't give in when others insisted I switch to English with them; it's a decision that has paid for itself thousands of times over.

The Jack Sparrow Method

Another issue you will deal with as a beginning learner is the amount of time you will likely spend *hesitating* during those first conversations in a new language. You might feel incredibly stupid if you're forced to pause, offering nothing but an "umm . . ." or "eehhh . . ." to the conversation.

This can make you feel uncomfortable, but it can also make the other person feel uncomfortable. It is one of the major reasons a conversation partner switches to your mother tongue with you; he or she does it out of kindness to "spare" you this discomfort.

If possible, such hesitations should be reduced or avoided. But this is much easier said than done! I remember someone writing a comment on YouTube about one of my videos—my first-ever attempt to use a language—telling me to "stop hesitating," as if it's as easy as that.

Hesitations are going to happen. We need this time to gather our thoughts, translate what we are thinking, remember a mnemonic or the word we want to say that's on the tip of our tongues, etc. Beginners are slower to speak, and that's just a fact of life; they will hesitate between saying the words they know. No one can just *stop* hesitating in this early stage.

But this doesn't mean that the awkwardness associated with the hesitation has to remain there. I have found that by hesitating in a different manner, I can remove some of the tension and awkwardness of the moment and make sure the person I'm speaking to feels comfortable, so our conversation can progress sufficiently.

A trick that has worked well, at least for my personality, is to add a little drama to these otherwise dull initial conversations. I remember the first time I saw the movie *Pirates of the Caribbean* and how Captain Jack Sparrow had an effective way of being dramatic through body language without saying a single word. It's an interesting concept; you maintain a person's attention by doing this. For instance, let's say you want to say a simple sentence like "I want to go to the supermarket," and you say "I want to go . . ." and the translation of "supermarket" just isn't coming to you in that instant. You need to think for a moment to remember what it is. What you could do then is hold up your index finger, look the person you're speaking to in the eye, to grab his or her attention, and then point off into the distance and stare there with a pensive look on your face. You will then have the undivided attention of that person, because you could be saying you want to go to . . . the airport, the desert, the dark side of the moon, the depths of the ocean, because you look like you are ready to go on a *quest*. With a bit of practice, you can get these dramatic pauses down to an art and do them automatically, while your mind races to think of what you would have otherwise been thinking—such as the elusive word for "supermarket."

You don't even have to be dramatic about it. Many orators make special use of pauses as they speak, which can actually make their speeches much more interesting. You don't have to produce a constant stream of words to hold a person's attention, but remember that by appearing nervous you may actually make the other person feel nervous. It's far better to try to enjoy yourself, or at least look like you're enjoying yourself, and then there will be no awkward pauses.

The Glass-Clink Trick

I remember hearing an "I'm too shy" excuse from a German woman I met in a bar in Berlin. I told her I had developed a wonderful technique to get over shyness called the glass-clink trick. I had piqued her curiosity and she wanted to know how it worked, so I walked toward the Americans she wanted to practice English with and told her to walk with me while I explained the complexity of how this advanced social technique worked. She was very interested indeed! I said, "The first step involves redistributing the blood around your body by raising your arm a little," and I grabbed the wrist of her hand holding a glass of Coke. She continued to listen attentively to this strange technique I was explaining, but by now we were moving just behind the Americans, and I took this chance of controlling her arm to extend it toward them to *clink* one of their glasses . . . and then I ran away! The Americans then turned around, saw an intriguing lady, waited for her to say something, and she mustered out a "Hello . . ." and a wonderful conversation began. Two hours later, she told me she had spent the whole evening practicing English with the Americans and was so proud of herself.

Of course, I explained to her that there was no special trick to getting over shyness, and my rambling was just to buy time until I had her in the right position to make the initial contact herself. All I did was move her arm muscles for her; the fact that she was in front of a group of native English speakers without any time to think herself out of talking to them meant that she had no choice but to start a conversation.

So next time a chance to use your target language with a native speaker comes up, consider my glass-clink trick—the only trick is to stop thinking yourself into shyness. Just approach the person and say hi. Shoot first and ask questions later, when it comes to talking to strangers. Remember that saying I mentioned in the previous chapter? "There are no strangers here, only friends you haven't yet met." When you speak to enough people, especially those who can encourage you in your target language, you start to appreciate how true this is.

Involve Me and I'll Understand

不闻不若闻之，闻之不若见之，见之不若知之，知之不若行之；学至于行之而止矣

Bù wén bú ruò wén zhī, wén zhī bú ruò jiàn zhī, jiàn zhī bú ruò zhīzhī, zhīzhī bú ruò xíng zhī; xué zhìyú xíng zhī ér zhǐ yǐ.

Tell me and I'll forget; show me and I may remember;
involve me and I'll understand.

—Chinese proverb

The best way to ensure progress and success in your language learning project is to be active from the start. Don't make your language learning all about studying; make it about *using* your target language.

If you walk up to someone (or use Skype), even if your dialogue lasts only ten seconds, you will have had your first-ever exchange in your target language and used the little you have learned. The next time, make it twenty seconds, then a minute, then five minutes, and so on to keep up this momentum.

Rather than study for some "ready" day that will never come, speak the language today.

- Find example sentences online, in a phrase book, or elsewhere and learn them. Just basic first-introduction dialogue is fine. Then use the suggestions in the previous chapter to find someone to practice them with.

- Maybe "cheat" by having a piece of paper with some words written on it you didn't have time yet to learn, or have a text document open if your first practice session is on your computer. Look things up in the middle of a conversation. It's okay; the person you're speaking with knows you are still learning.

- When you have enough words and phrases to start with, find ways to rephrase what you may want to say with alternative words. Be imaginative.

- In your spoken sessions, keep talking despite mistakes, and rather than going through a language course designed to try to teach you "everything," make your study sessions relevant to your spoken sessions.

- Consider dabbling in Esperanto for two weeks, so that you don't have to worry about exceptions or tough vocabulary, and get used to the feeling of speaking and using a new language, in general, which will give your confidence a boost for your target language. A free Esperanto course is available online at Lernu.net, and much more information about Esperanto is accessible at fi3m.com/esperanto.

- Try to keep your conversations in that target language, make inevitable hesitations more fun, and try not to think too much. I like the Lonely Planet's phrase book motto: "Don't just stand there, say something!" It's okay to struggle, as long as you are saying *something*. Communication is always the point.

For videos, links, and more information relevant to this chapter, see fi3m.com/ch–5.

CHAPTER 6

Tips for Starting Specific Languages

> Learning a specific language is easier than you think. Here I tell you why.

Up until now, everything in this book can be applied to learning any language. The communicative approach, philosophies, and guidelines I suggest have worked for me and many language learners for many years. I have even applied my speak-from-day-one approach to learning sign language (of course with a basic terminology adjustment of *sign* from day one) and learned to communicate in ASL (American Sign Language) in the same way I have in Chinese, Irish, French, Spanish, and many other languages.

Having said that, when we take on specific languages there are indeed tricks you can apply to give you an extra edge. In this chapter, I discuss these advantages and apply them to the

language you might be taking on. I also offer lots of encouragement, especially for languages that have been traditionally
viewed as difficult.

Before I get into listing each linguistic family and particular
languages within them, I want to introduce a few terms and
concepts that will help you here.

Cognates

A *cognate* is a word that not only looks and sounds like a word we
already know, but it also means the same thing we know it to
mean in our mother tongue as it does in our target language.

No matter what language you are learning, you will find that
some international words tend to be the same, albeit with a
localized pronunciation. "Obama," for instance, as with most
proper names, is the same in every language you will come
across. Brand names also tend to be very similar across languages, such as Coca-Cola (even in Mandarin, where it's *Kekou-
Kele,* ignoring tone marks).

There are also cognates that aren't spelled exactly the same,
but it doesn't take a feat of imagination to make the connection,
such as *posesión* in Spanish and "possession" in English.

There are exceptions, of course. In Mandarin, Pepsi (Cola) is
actually called *Baishi (Kele),* for instance. Rather than expect all
cognates in a particular category to be familiar, it's better to use
these cognate tips as a guideline for finding words that are likely
to be similar or the same. You can double-check them when

necessary, but the point is that you will effectively have no need to work at remembering this type of word because you already know it, or a close form of it. The only trick is to get used to its slightly different pronunciation, which is good training for getting used to the sound of that language anyway. Use it a few times and you will know this word.

Essentially, cognates are heaps of free vocabulary, and they are one reason it is impossible to start a language truly "from scratch." *Sushi*, to cite one example, is almost always "sushi" everywhere you go in the world. All across Europe, the words for "democracy" and "communism" have pronunciations so similar to their English equivalents, you'd almost have to try hard *not* to recognize them.

In particular professional fields, cognates are much more common than in others. While some vocabulary is likely to be quite different across languages, words related to technology, on the other hand, may be incredibly similar. In Italian, you turn on your *computer*, and in Brazilian Portuguese, you move the *mouse*. In Russian, you connect to the Интернет (an exact translitera-tion of "Internet," where И = I, н = n, and p = r), and in Japanese, you check your Eメール (*mē-ru*, Japanese's transliteration of "e-mail"). The name of the program you may use to surf the Internet in Turkish is *Firefox*, and you may be doing so in *Micro-soft Windows* in the Somali language, on an *Apple* in Tagalog, or in *Linux* in Basque.

As well as brand names, you also have food or other cultural nuggets that are associated with a particular place, originally

English, or from another language. The Czech word *robot* tends to be used in most languages, and Italian foods (*pizza, pasta, gnocchi*) are adapted in many places.

Listing all cognates for a given language is beyond the scope of this book, but brand names, technology words, and even some trendy words (like *cool* in both French and German) are more likely to be international.

One of the first things I do when I am learning a language is find a list of these cognates or similar-looking words. These lists can contain hundreds or even thousands of examples. Refer to them as soon as possible, no matter what language you are learning, and I'll share some typical examples in the next section.

Conjugations

Modal verbs are "helper" verbs (action words) that help us to express a concept, without having to worry so much about the grammar of conjugation. You may remember this concept, which was introduced briefly in the previous chapter.

Conjugation is how words change depending on who is doing the action. So, in English, for the verb "to be" we have "I am," "you are, " and "he/she/it is." Conjugation also affects the verb tense, indicating the time the action takes place: "I am" (present tense) becomes "I will be" (future tense) and "I was" (past tense). If there were no conjugation in English, then we would use "be" in place of "am," "are," "is," "will be," and "was." (This is how it works in some Asian languages, such as Chinese.)

Learners of English are lucky in that English conjugation is relatively simple most of the time. In the present tense, you often add an s ("I eat" versus "he eats," "I jog" versus "he jogs"). Unfortunately, for many European languages this is not the case. The Spanish *contar* ("to tell"), for instance, becomes *cuento* ("I tell"), *contamos* ("we tell"), and *contaste* ("you told"), which are quite different from one another. This conjugation is pretty standard across Spanish, and the vowel change is easier to get used to than you think, but if you're an absolute beginner, it can slow you down.

That's why I recommend using helper verbs. Just learn the conjugation of a few verbs and tack on the dictionary form to the end of them. Instead of saying "I will tell," which would require you to think of future-tense conjugations, you can rephrase it as "I want to tell," as discussed in chapter 5. In Spanish, you only have to remember that "I want" is *quiero*, and you very easily get *quiero contar*, and can replace any other action word in place of "tell" in the same way.

With any language, I suggest learning the following modal verbs:

can (able to)
should
would like to
must / have to
want to

Since my conversations tend to be mostly one-on-one as a beginner, the "I" and "you" (singular) conjugations are my first priority. After this, I start to use "we," then "he/she/it" and "them." (Generally, "he/she/it" verb forms, known as the third-person singular, follow the same conjugation pattern in many languages.)

Many languages have both polite and informal personal pronoun forms, which may sound complicated, but to simplify things, I suggest you focus on the polite form of "you" and ignore the more intimate alternative, at least at first. It sounds weird to refer to a close friend or a young person with the polite form in many countries, but if you plan to use the language with strangers, it's better to go with this form. When you start to feel a little comfortable in the language, learn the alternative and try to switch between them appropriately.

Romance Languages

Let's begin with *Romance languages*! That is to say, French, Spanish, Portuguese, and Italian (as well as Romanian, Catalan, Galician, Sardinian, Corsican, and many others). These all descended from vulgar Latin, the language spoken across the Roman Empire. They have a huge number of cognates in common with one another, but here I want to discuss the cognates they have in common with English.

You see, even though English is not a Romance language, since England was occupied by the Normans in 1066, the aristocrats and royalty in England spoke Norman French for several centuries after that. This meant a huge influx of Norman

French vocabulary came into English, the majority of which resembles modern French and other Romance languages.

The trick is recognizing which words to use, and when you know the context in which English "borrowed" these words, this becomes a lot easier.

Aristocrats are more likely to use formal vocabulary, and the English equivalents of these words tend to be more French-like. So when speaking any of these Romance languages, think of a formal alternative to that word in English and this may indeed be the same in your target language. For instance, if someone knocks on your door, you might tell that person to "come in," or you could say "enter." In French, it's *entrer*; Spanish, *entrar*. If you want to share your thoughts with someone, you tell your "point of view," share your "opinion," or give this person your "perspective." In Italian, *opinione*; in Portuguese, *perspectiva*. Although here, *point de vue* in French is also not far off. Instead of showing someone a city, you could be the person's "guide," which is the same word used in French: *guide*. Learning vocabulary can be easy, but it's better when it's "simple" (which is the same in both French and Spanish: *simple*).

"Enter," "opinion," and "simple," compared to "come in," "thoughts," and "easy," are words I might use in more formal situations in English—like in a job interview or in a debate—but they are not words I would use at a party, for instance. There, they would seem a little pompous. But in Romance languages, these words are quite commonly used. With practice, you learn to rephrase a sentence in your head *and* look for alternative words for what you want to say. Doing so in Romance languages gives you an edge in many situations.

More specifically, though, words of a particular type or ending are much more likely to be cognates. For instance, words that end in "-tion" in English are very likely to be the same in French, albeit with a French pronunciation. In Spanish, the ending becomes -ción; in Italian, it's -zione; and in Portuguese, -ção. There are plenty of words like this: action, application, communication, destruction, fiction, frustration, information, inspiration, invention, invitation, nation, option, perfection, population, protection, solution, tradition, and many, many more.

There's also "-tude" (gratitude, magnitude), "-sion" (explosion, expression), "-ment" (encouragement, segment), "-age" (garage, camouflage), and loads more. Granted, you'll find the occasional "false friend," whose meaning may be subtly or very different, but in general you can rely on these to increase your vocabulary within an incredibly short period of time.

As well as these recognizable words and endings, a branch of Romance-based words relate to similar English words and, though they may be spelled differently, give you a familiar starting point. From "communication," we get the French verb communiquer ("to communicate"). From "information," we get the Spanish informar ("to inform"; used more frequently than the equivalent in English). From "encouragement," giving us incoraggiamento, we also get Italian's incoraggiare: "to encourage."

Spanish

Spanish is a very straightforward language in that it is phonetic (each letter has one sound in every situation, with a few exceptions like *ch*, *ll*, and *u* after *g* and *q*), and it is one of the easier languages when it comes to remembering what the gender of words is, as they tend to end with an *a* for the feminine and an *o* for the masculine. Exceptions to this (such as *-ma* being masculine in *el problema*) are listed in most language courses. If you aren't sure, just use the masculine form, as this is not a mistake that hinders communication.

One slightly trickier feature of Spanish is its complex conjugation system. This isn't as bad as it seems at first glance, because Spanish follows very easy-to-recognize patterns (an *o* may change to a *ue* when that syllable is stressed in the word, for instance). Before getting used to these conjugations, though, a beginner should probably focus on using modal verbs followed by the dictionary (infinitive) version of a verb as often as possible to be more confident that the sentence is correct, while always keeping in mind that it's okay to make a few mistakes here and there.

Some Spanish modal verbs worth knowing are in the list below. Note that you can add an *s* to the polite "he/she/it/you" forms shown here to get the informal "you" forms, or add an *n* to them to get the "they" verb form. Remember that when there is no written accent or consonant other than *s* or *n* at the end, the stress will always be on the second-to-last syllable, so it's *puedo*, but then *podemos*.

....

poder: to be able, can, may

puedo   I can

puede   he/she/it/you (polite) can

podemos   we can

....

querer: to want

quiero   I want

quiere   he/she/it/you (polite) want(s)

queremos   we want

....

tener que: to have to

tengo que   I have to

tiene que   he/she/it/you (polite) has/have to

tenemos que we have to

....

deber: should, must

debo   I should

debe   he/she/it/you (polite) should

debemos   we should

....

A future verb tense is also very easily represented by "go to" and in many cases can be replaced with the future conjugation for a somewhat similar meaning.

....

ir a: to go to

voy a   I am going to

| va a | he/she/it/you (polite) is/are going to |
| vamos a | We are going to |

....

For more tips on Spanish, see fi3m.com/spanish.

French

French is one of the most familiar languages to an English speaker when it comes to its written form, because it has more cognates that don't require any spelling alterations than any other language. Rather than the French borrowing terms from English, as with some of the cognate examples I gave previously, we English speakers have borrowed from them!

The "liaison" between words and how they are pronounced when they are together in a sentence does take a little getting used to (you *do* pronounce the first s—as a z—in *les arbres* but not in *les pommes*), but people who know you're learning will follow you, thanks to the context, even if you get this sort of thing wrong. It may seem tricky, but French is in fact much more phonetic and consistent than English, so once you get used to this new system, it's incredibly reliable.

Remembering whether a noun is masculine or feminine can also seem difficult, but this tends to follow very clear patterns based on the ending of a word:

- Generally, words that end in a consonant (other than *n, s, t,* and *x*) are almost always masculine, such as *franc, lac, bord, pied, shampooing, detail, travail, soleil.*

- Words that end in -*asion, -sion, -tion, -xion* are almost always feminine, such as *liaison, maison, raison, décision, tension, vision, connexion*.

- If a word ends in an *e*, it's slightly more likely to be feminine, such as *façade, salade, ambulance, thèse, fontaine*.

- Exceptions include those words ending in -*isme* (*tourisme*), -*ède, -ège, -ème* (*problème, poème, système*), and -*age* (*courage, garage, message, voyage*).

This list will help you guess most of the time what gender a word is, and once you become more familiar with it, I would recommend *not worrying about it too much*. I guarantee French speakers will understand you just fine if you say *le table blanc* instead of the correct *la table blanche* ("the white table"). This will not hinder communication as a beginner. It's more important to fix this in the later stages of your learning process, when you concentrate more on speaking correctly.

Next, conjugation in French can be difficult to get used to, but unlike most other Romance languages, the personal pronoun (I, you, he/she/it) is always included, which means getting the conjugation right is even less of a priority for beginners, since you always know *who* is being referred to.

Another way you can get a head start is to learn one less conjugation, because *on* ("one," as in "one does not like this") is used very frequently in place of *nous* ("we"). Plus, you use the same conjugation for "you" singular (polite) as you do for "you" plural conjugation, and most of the time the conjugation for "you" singular (informal) is the same as for "I" (*je*), but with an s added that is usually not even pronounced. *Je mange* and *tu manges.*

In the following examples, despite the different spellings, the first and second conjugations tend to be pronounced exactly the same (*peux/peut, veux/veut*), and in the first three examples, the *tu* conjugation (the informal "you," which I've not included) is the same as the *je* one (*peux, veux,* and *dois*).

Try to keep these modal verbs in mind, as you can immediately follow them with a dictionary form of a verb (action word):

pouvoir:	*to be able, can, may*
je peux	*I can*
il/elle/on peut	*he/she/one can*
vous pouvez	*you (polite) can*

vouloir:	*to want*
je veux	*I want*
il/elle/on veut	*he/she/one want(s)*
vous voulez	*you (polite) want*

devoir:	*to have to, should*
je dois	*I have to*
il/elle/on doit	*he/she/it/one has to*
vous devez	*you (polite) have to*

A future verb tense is also very easily represented by "go to" (in the sense of intention, not movement) and can, in many cases, be replaced with the future conjugation for a somewhat similar meaning.

aller:	to go to
je vais	I am going to
il/elle/on va	he/she/one is going to
vous allez	you (polite) are going to

For much more on French, see fi3m.com/french.

Italian

Italian is another phonetic language, although a few letter-combination pronunciations take some getting used to, such as ci, ce, and gl. As in Spanish, feminine words tend to end with an a, masculine words with an o, apart from similar exceptions mentioned in most courses.

As with the other languages, learning some modal verbs can help you create complete sentences much more easily:

potere:	to be able, can
posso	I can
può	he/she/it/you (polite) can
possiamo	we can

....

volere:	*to want*
voglio	*I want*
vuole	*he/she/it/you (polite) want(s)*
vogliamo	*we want*

....

dovere:	*should, have to, must*
devo	*I should*
deve	*he/she/it/you (polite) should*
dobbiamo	*we should*

....

Follow these with an action verb in its dictionary (infinitive) form, such as *voglio trovare* for "I want to find." To include the future tense in any discussion, just use the standard present form of the verb paired with a time (*domani* for "tomorrow," for instance), and this will be correct Italian in most cases.

For more tips on Italian, see fi3m.com/italian.

Portuguese

Portuguese is also very phonetic and similar to Spanish in the way you recognize noun genders.

Fortunately, you need only three conjugations (at least in most Brazilian Portuguese dialects) to cover all possibilities, because the third person covers he/she, you, and we. The third person is rendered as *a gente,* similar to French's *on* ("one," as in "one does not like this"). When using this form, it's best to place the *a gente* before the conjugation, such as *a gente pode*.

The following can be quite useful conjugations to learn:

....

poder: *to be able, can, may*

posso *I can*

pode *he/she/it/you/one can*

podem *they can*

....

querer: *to want*

quero *I want*

quer *he/she/it/you/one want(s)*

querem *they want*

....

ter que: *to have to*

tenho que *I have to*

tem que *he/she/it/you/one has/have to*

têm que *they have to*

....

For much more on Portuguese, see fi3m.com/portuguese.

Germanic Languages

A little closer to home, we have the Germanic languages. This is the branch of the linguistic family on which our own English rests. As such, there are a lot of things we share in common with German, Dutch, Norwegian, Icelandic, Danish, Swedish, and Afrikaans.

Unlike English, however, these languages tend to be very much phonetic, in that the spelling and pronunciation rules (apart from borrowed English words, which are more common than you think) are consistent. Those rules may be different than what you are used to, but once you learn them, you can generally pronounce any word that you see spelled out.

Endless remnants of what German and English have in common crop up often, and the grammar feels eerily familiar, especially for anyone who has read Shakespeare. Several hundred years ago, English's "you" was actually the plural version of the word that is today's all-encompassing singular and plural "you." "Thou" is not that far off the sound of today's German and Norwegian *du*. And "thine" compares with the German *dein*. From "thee" we have *dich*. Even the conjugation follows the same pattern of "Thou hast," *Du hast*. Keeping this in mind has helped German conjugation feel a little more familiar to me.

But where these Germanic languages start to make more sense is in their common vocabulary.

As always, for whatever language you are learning, make sure to find a list of cognates. In German/Dutch/Swedish, "apple" is *Apfel/appel/apple*, "arm" and "April" are both exactly the same in all three languages, "foot" is *Fuß/voet/fot*, and "book" is *Buch/boek/bok* (in the two latter examples, *oe* is the *oo* sound in Dutch). There are countless others.

In this case, you can actually apply the *opposite* advice from the Romance languages section, where I mention considering more formal words in English to find possible cognates. With these languages, find *less formal* words—not slang though, as the words need to be more likely a part of older English. So, while French and Spanish have *entrer* and *entrar* to resemble our "enter," the alternative of "come in" also has Germanic equivalents. In German, it's *(her)einkommen*. Rather than use a word like "consider," if you opt for "think (about)," you'll find that *denken* is "think" in German and Dutch. Generally, words for parts of the body, many animals, and tools tend to be quite similar or even exactly the same.

While we certainly have lots in common, Germanic languages are also slightly more likely than other languages to borrow words from English. You'll find these among any lists of cognates.

In German, for instance, *Flat Rate* is used to describe cell-phone contracts. There's also *Interview* (in the context of a TV or celebrity interview), *cool* (as in "great," not cold temperatures), *Jeans, Jetlag, Job, Musical, Party, Sandwich, Scanner, Toast, Top Ten, unfair, Website,* and many others. If the German word associated with technology or something trendy, it may be possible to use the English word, but you can confirm this in a list of cognates.

Germanic languages also borrow words from other languages English has borrowed from, such as *Restaurant, Charme, Cousin, Dessert, Hotel, Omelette, Prinz, Tourist, Zigarette,* and many other words from French that are recognizable even with slight spelling changes, and this also applies to Dutch, Norwegian, etc.

German

German applies three genders to nouns, (masculine, feminine, and neuter), which at first can seem totally randomly assigned. Of course, this is not the case. Although the meaning of the word (apart from any people or animals associated with that gender) does not contribute so much, it's the ending of the word you need to look at, and remember it's the word that has gender, not the object. For example,

- the endings -ant, -ast, -ich, -ig, -ismus, -ling, -or, -us are masculine,

- -a, -anz, -ei, -enz, -heit, -ie, -ik, -in, -keit, -schaft, -sion, -sis, -tion, tät, -ung, -ur are feminine, and

- -chen, -icht, -il, -it, -lein, -ma, -ment, -tel, -tum, -um are neuter.

- Apart from this, words ending in -el, -er, -en are mostly masculine, those ending in -t or -e are mostly feminine, and those with the prefix Ge- are mostly neuter.

This may seem incredibly intimidating, but it's a small enough list that you *can* learn it, and it will cover the vast majority of words you are likely to come across so that you will know their likely gender as soon as you see or hear them. This is much more efficient than trying to learn the gender of every single word individually. There are some exceptions and words not covered by these descriptions, but whenever you can't be confident of a word's gender, *just guess*. A one in three chance is fine and it won't be the end of the world if you get it wrong. As always, it won't confuse a German to hear you say *der Auto* when it's actually *das Auto*. Fix gender issues later in your language learning story, but keep the previous examples in mind so you have a lot less work to do to learn those genders.

German grammar can also seem intimidating with all the terminology used in grammar books, such as *accusative, dative, nominative,* and *genitive,* but I find that learning sentences and seeing how words come up in context makes grammar much easier to deal with. Certain words follow particular prepositions *all* the time, for instance.

These *grammatical cases* are comparable to how, in English, we distinguish between "I" and "me," or "he" and "him." You use one for the subject ("I"; *ich* in German) and one for the object ("me"; *mich* in German). German just expands on this to add a new one (*mir*) in certain situations, but I never found that people misunderstood me if I got these mixed up when I was starting to speak German.

Conjugation in German is harder than in English but still less complex than in the Romance languages. Nearly all the time *ich* ("I") has an -*e* ending, *du* ("you") has an -*st* ending, "he/she/it" has a -*t* ending, and "we/they" has an -*en*. Even so, to give your sentences more versatility, it's still very useful to learn modal verbs first. There are six modal verbs (*dürfen, mögen, sollen, können, müssen, wollen*), all of which are irregular, but I got more mileage out of focusing on the following ones first:

....

können: *to be able, can*

ich/er/sie kann   *I/he/she can*

wir/sie können   *we/you (polite) can*

....

mögen: *would like to**

ich/er/sie möchte   *I/he/she would like to*

wir/sie möchten   *we/you (polite) would like to*

> ** Used mostly in Konjunktiv II (subjunctive II)*
> *form; a less commonly used normal form*
> *not mentioned here means "may"*

....

müssen: *have to, must*

ich/er/sie muss   *I/he/she have/has to*

wir/sie müssen   *we/you (polite) has/have to*

....

wollen: *to want*

ich/er/sie will   *I/he/she wants*

wir/sie wollen   *we/you (polite) want*

....

Add -st to the first form of each of these to get the informal "you," or just -t if it already ends in s.

For many more tips on German, check out fi3m.com/german.

Slavic Languages

While I certainly can't speak for *mastering* Slavic languages, I have experience reaching the conversational level in Czech. I've also dabbled in other Slavic languages, like Polish, and I understand rudimentary Russian. Some of the tips in the following paragraphs may also apply to other Slavic languages, including Slovakian, Ukrainian, and Serbo-Croatian.

The most intimidating aspect when you start to learn these languages tends to be grammar. Each language features many grammatical cases, which makes it seem as though you have to learn six or seven different versions of each word—or twelve or fourteen, when you include plural forms.

These are, however, usually predictable changes to the ends of words. Rather than learning the rules, you'll get used to them with enough exposure. I actually got by quite well using the basic dictionary (nominative) forms of words as a beginner and people continued to understand me, and I slowly expanded on that. As with all languages, it's okay to utter a few mistakes— native speakers are very forgiving.

It's common to overlook aspects of these languages that can make them much easier to learn. They are almost always very phonetic, once again with consistent spelling and pronunciation rules (compared to English's mess of words, like though, through, plough, dough, cough). When you see a word, you know precisely how it should be pronounced, and vice versa, whether with those that use Latin script or those that use Cyrillic, such as Russian.

Slavic languages may not offer the same similar-words advantage the Romance or Germanic languages do when it comes to learning new vocabulary, but they do tend to be very logically consistent in how they construct words. This means that when you learn a manageable set of prepositions and prefixes plus word roots, you can discover a lot of new words.

For instance, let's take the four prefixes in Czech: *v, vy, od,* and *za.* In their prefix form, add them to a word root—the central part of a word—*chod,* for instance, which is related to the verb *chodit* ("to go"). By itself, and as a prefix in many verbs, *v* means "in," so for "go in" you have *vchod,* which means "entrance"! *Vý/vy* doesn't exist by itself in this context, but it means the opposite, and you have "exit": *východ. Od* by itself means "from," so what do you think a "from-go" thing would be? A "departure": *odchod!*

It isn't always this logical, but you can create a small story in your head for when it isn't, to help you remember the meaning of a word. *Záchod,* for instance, is "toilet" in Czech. The prefix-preposition *za* tends to mean "behind" or "off," so I imagined excusing myself and "leaving" where I was to go to the bathroom.

Ultimately, if you understand even vaguely the meanings associated with the prefixes *do, na, nad(e), ne, o(b), od(e), pa, po, popo, pod, pro, pře, před, při, roz, s(e), spolu, u, v(e), vy, vz, z,* and *za,* then you have the building blocks to form many words and understand what words mean the first time you see them. While these examples are in Czech, you will find the methods can be applied similarly to other Slavic languages.

This verb *chtít* ("to want") can be among the more useful ones in forming sentences while being able to use its dictionary form:

chtít:	*to want*
chci	*I want*
chce	*he/she/it wants*
chceme	*we want*

You can also take this verb and use the conditional tense conjugation to express "would like" by adding *chtěl* before the conditional mood, which is simply: *bych* ("I would"), *bys* ("you would"), *by* ("he/she/it would"), *bychom* ("we would"), *byste* ("you [plural] would"), *by* ("they would"). This conditional can be added after any verb in its dictionary form, if making it conditional would help you simplify your sentence in some way.

Other modal verbs worth learning the conjugation of include *moct* (to be able, can), *umět* (to know how), *muset* (must, have to), *smět* (be allowed to), and *mít* (to have to).

Arabic

Having reached a conversational (lower intermediate, B1) level in Egyptian Arabic, I would recommend that those with a *spoken* focus choose a specific Arabic dialect they have a preference for based on the country they would like to visit most.

Modern Standard Arabic (MSA), which most courses tend to focus on, is essential if you want to read newspapers and books or watch or listen to news broadcasts. But dialects, in every country, tend to be much more useful for conversing with people in the street or understanding most Arabic movies and TV shows. Dialects are also much easier to learn.

While MSA is definitely useful, its grammar is much more complex than a dialect's, which can slow down a beginner's progress. Grammar is easy to pick up, however, once you're familiar with the language.

For instance, the word "house" in "The house is there," "I put it in the house," or "I like this house" is always going to be *bayt* in Egyptian dialect, but it would be *baytu*, *bayta*, and *bayti* respectively in MSA because of how the word operates in different "cases" in each sentence.

With all this in mind, you can get dialect-focused lessons or exchanges, as I've mentioned in previous chapters, or find small phrase books tailored to the dialect you want to learn, and study this material between spoken sessions. Once you are confident in your spoken abilities in your dialect, it's much easier to come back to the more complex MSA.

Now, as for using modal verbs, unlike the other languages listed so far, this is not as easy a work-around in Arabic because the second verb is still altered depending on who it refers to. Arabic verb conjugation is actually very straightforward and logical, although it is a little different from what we are used to in other languages.

After some practice using this with a native, it turns out to not be that bad after all. Even the new script isn't too bad, as I mention in the next section.

For some tips on Egyptian Arabic and other Arabic dialects, as well as MSA, and which resources may help, see fi3m.com/arabic.

Phonetic Script

A language that doesn't use the same written alphabet as the one you are reading now can seem very intimidating. However, languages like Arabic, Russian, Korean, Greek, Thai, and others that use a phonetic script essentially require that you learn only a small set of characters, which represent particular sounds, and doing so will allow you to read that language as you would read any western European language.

Using a familiar writing system (as with many European languages) tends to make us biased toward pronouncing all words the way we would in our mother tongue. This is one reason we hang on to bad pronunciations longer than we should. This won't be a problem for you with phonetic languages, because you'll learn a new sound correctly *from the start* without any bias.

As with any language, I like to use a little association (which is as visual as possible) when doing this. After a few examples, you'll see what I mean and you can continue this process to apply associations to your target language's script.

For instance, this is the Thai character that represents the *ah* sound: ๅ

It doesn't look anything like a European *a*, but I got a great suggestion from polyglot Stu Jay Raj when I was learning Thai. He suggested that you imagine a man peeing against a tree; the path that his pee takes represents that of this letter, and the sound he makes on relieving himself is of course *aaaaah*. This is a visual story that is easy to remember and associate with the character. I generally go for more graphic or silly images like this to help me remember new letters.

Next, this is the Arabic letter that represents the *b* sound: ب

Rather than a complex visual image, all I had to remember was that the dot was below the line. *Below* has the *b* sound—problem solved!

In the same way, ت is the *t* sound because there are t̲w̲o̲ dots above the line, and ث is the *th* sound because there are t̲h̲r̲ee dots. For other letters, you have to get more visual, though. So with م I imagined a mouse with his tail hanging loose or connecting to the next letter, since this is the *m* sound.

All it really takes is one afternoon of sitting down with a new alphabet in front of you and thinking of things that help you visually recognize each character. It might take a few hours to go through the entire alphabet, but this will be time very well invested. You require that visual association at first while you read, and this certainly slows you down, but you get used to it and eventually *know* what the sound is instantly. Then you can discard the visual association, like you would training wheels on a bike.

Memrise.com can be a useful resource here, as it has mnemonics prepared for various alphabets.

Tonal Languages

When it comes to languages like Thai, Mandarin, Cantonese, or Vietnamese, many people quickly say they could never speak these because their *tones* make them too hard. Many claim they are tone deaf and could never manage to process them. I find this strange, because even if the person claiming this is *musically* tone deaf, that person can still fully interpret the prosody and intonation of speech in his or her native language.

We have tones in English and other European languages; we just apply them to indicate subtle differences in the meanings of words and sentences rather than using them to change the core meaning of a word (although this is also possible). We can all tell the difference between "Oh?" when said as a question to show a curiosity for more details (the tone goes from low to high) and "Oh . . ." disappointingly said to show feeling let down by the information heard (the tone is shorter and lowers briefly). The sounds of both of these serve to convey how the word should be understood.

It definitely takes practice for those of us not used to incorporating tones so specifically into our learning process or applying them to languages to convey differences in meaning. Time with a native speaker, and going through it slowly while repeating what that person says a few times, can help you adapt to these. Anyone dedicated to it can learn tones relatively quickly, and then they become second nature.

Despite the fact that tones distinguish meanings of words, people still understand me regularly even when I fail to use the right ones thanks to the context of the sentence, and the fact that they adjust to me as a learner. The more I say, despite using incorrect tones on several words, the more context I provide and the listener can adjust to see what I mean.

When I arrived in Taiwan, I spoke only Mandarin outside the house, and despite needing several weeks before feeling more confident with my tones, I ordered food, asked directions, and was understood by those not used to speaking with foreigners. They understood what I meant from the context, and what tone I meant, similar to the way that you'd understand me if I asked you for "the wee to the leebry" on the street—wrong pronunciation indeed, but very likely to mean "the way to the library," especially with plenty of context.

Like with everything else in language learning, attitude is the key. Rather than lament over how *impossible tones are*, you just throw yourself at the problem and solve it. I gave tones my full dedication during the first weeks of learning Mandarin, instead of spreading myself thin trying to learn too many things at once. This helped me get ahold on them more quickly for the rest of my learning process.

You saw in chapter 3, with my *mùbiāo* example, how I learn vocabulary in tonal languages, by incorporating a visual aspect of falling or going straight or bouncing or flying up, depending on the appropriate tone. Others have used colors to help them make tone associations. I also tried singing out sentences and recording videos to track my progress. Though this took a lot of work, it was nowhere near as difficult as so many made it out to be.

It's not about mastering tones in your first week or two but just making sure you are doing them well enough to be understood. Then, as you practice, you can continue to improve your skills. Consistent time with native speakers will show you how tones aren't as bad as you think.

Chinese

Chinese is one of the most notorious languages around, and many claim that it's the hardest in the world. This is usually based on nothing more than seeing Chinese script, in which you have to learn a completely new complex character for "every single word."

Don't take these scare tactics to heart! First, keep in mind that *Chinese* is a broad term, encompassing many varieties as well as the writing system, but you may want to narrow down your work to Mandarin, Cantonese, or some other specific variety if your focus is more spoken.

I decided to temporarily put aside learning how to read Chinese so I could focus on speaking Mandarin. Reaching the conversational level in that language in a few months became much more realistic. Then, when I was a more confident speaker,

I got back into the language from the perspective of improving my reading skills. It was much easier than when I'd tried before, because I had a better sense of how the language worked and a firmer understanding of the meaning of the words when sounded out.

Learning new vocabulary when you already have some basics is actually much more logical than it is in many European languages. For instance, *jiǎn zhèn qì* means "shock absorber" in Mandarin. With a small amount of knowledge, this word, which may initially seem intimidating, can be quite easy to decipher. *Jiǎn*, for instance, means "to reduce." (*Jiǎnféi* means "to lose weight" [reduce fat] and *jiǎn jià* means "sale" [reduce price].) *Qì*, a very common everyday word, means "tool" or "device." Even if you don't recognize that *zhèn* means "to shake," you can still deduce that it's a *tool* for *reducing* something, which is a lot of help!

In general, new words are very easy to understand when you look at their components in this way.

When you are ready to read Chinese, it may seem as if there are too many characters to process, but keep in mind that a smaller number of frequent ones are used a lot and with just five hundred you will already recognize 80 percent of the characters you read and certainly those on most menus and signs. With a good mnemonics system, and when you are already used to speaking the language *first,* you can focus on this better and progress in it very quickly.

When I was learning how to read, I used my trusted keyword method to help me learn vocabulary. For simple characters, this is quite easy. "Big," 大, actually looks like a person stretching out his or her arms to say how big something is, but for more complex characters you need a little more context. One way to do this is to learn as many of the *radicals* (building blocks of each character) as you can and build up a meaning from them. Some of these meanings are logical, such as "home" being 家 because it's a "pig" under a "roof," and in older times a home would have had an animal in it.

Some are not so immediately logical and require imagination to connect their building blocks. Many books are available that go through characters systematically, explaining why they mean certain things. When using these, keep in mind that it is more efficient to focus on the most frequent characters rather than try to go from beginning to end.

As a vegetarian trying to understand menus, for instance, I discovered one thing that helped me immensely. Many vegetables have the same radical above them that implies it's a vegetable or is grass-related. "Spinach" is 菠菜, "green onion" is 葱, "tomato" is 蕃茄, "potato" is 薯, "aubergine (eggplant)" is 茄子, "lettuce" is 莴苣, and so on.

Can you see the same fence-like component on the top of each character? Character formations are far from random, and there are consistencies throughout that help you to learn them faster.

For much more encouragement related to learning Chinese, see fi3m.com/chi.

Japanese

Japanese is another language that intimidates many would-be learners, but don't let the naysayers fool you! Like all languages, it has many aspects to it that actually make it easier than others. Many Westerners have successfully learned the language, so you can too, if you are dedicated.

Learning kanji (Chinese characters used in Japanese) is likely the most intimidating part of learning the language. But there's good news: what I said about learning characters in Chinese applies equally to Japanese. A small number of frequent kanji accounts for the vast majority of the language you are likely to encounter day to day. For example, just fewer than two hundred characters account for 50 percent of all kanji used on Japanese Wikipedia, while just fewer than five hundred characters account for 75 percent.

Japanese has three phonetic alphabets (Hiragana, Katakana, and Romaji), which will allow you to start reading Japanese before you know even a single kanji. Many Japanese learner materials are written in Romaji, which can be learned almost instantly (it's how Japanese words are rendered in the Latin alphabet), while most Japanese children's books are written completely in Hiragana, and there are lots of very familiar borrowed words written in Katakana, both of which can be learned in a weekend. And if learner texts and children's books aren't your thing, many manga (Japanese comic books) and news sites like NHK News Web Easy add little Hiragana reading guides next to kanji so you can start reading real Japanese no matter your level of kanji knowledge.

Pronunciation in Japanese is among its easiest aspects. The language has an extremely small number of sounds, almost all of which are found in Romance languages. And you will be happy to know that Japanese sounds are one-to-one, meaning each Hiragana, Katakana, or Romaji sound can be pronounced only one way! For example, the Japanese sound *e* (written え in Hiragana and エ in Katakana) is always pronounced the exact same way no matter what word it appears in, unlike the English letter *e*, which has numerous different pronunciations, as shown in the words "bet," "beer," "alert," "here," "there," etc.).

Even better, Japanese is not a tonal language, so you don't have to produce the proper tone for each syllable (like you do in Mandarin) to be understood. Japanese does have some high–low distinctions (e.g., *hashi* pronounced high–low means "chopsticks" while it means "bridge" when pronounced low–high), but these distinctions are fairly small in number and the context will almost always make it clear which word is being referred to. Regardless, learning kanji eliminates any potential ambiguity.

Another major advantage Japanese offers native speakers of English is the large number of borrowed English words used. When in doubt, you can try to say an English word using Japanese pronunciation and you may be completely understood!

Granted, there are indeed some challenging aspects to the language, but like everything, you get used to them if you get exposure, use the language, stay motivated, and keep pushing yourself to learn all the time.

For much more information to help you on your Japanese mission, see fi3m.com/japanese.

Irish (Gaeilge)

The language of my own country, Irish, is worth mentioning too, of course! Note that Irish, or Gaeilge, is the standard name for the Celtic language of Ireland (not to be confused with Gaelic, the language of Scotland); our dialect of English is actually referred to as Hiberno English, or "Irish English"— never "Irish."

Irish intimidated me as a learner in school, but not because of its inherent difficulty as much as its presentation to us in school, which has luckily improved in recent years. In fact, it is a beautiful language, which you can really enjoy learning. Unlike other European languages, it has only eleven irregular verbs (others typically have hundreds, or even thousands, depending on how you count them).

One aspect of Irish that people may complain about is that it is a harder language to practice. In fact, Irish is an official language of the European Union, and there are multiple streamed radio stations and TV shows you can watch for free online. You could spend your entire day getting bombarded with several options to expose yourself to Irish. There are also online discussion groups, and if you make it to Ireland, the wonderful Gaeltacht regions have many tens of thousands of people using Irish as their main language throughout the day.

The phonetic system can seem intimidating, but it's actually quite logical. Celtic languages change the beginning of words; English, in contrast, changes only the middle (like "man" versus "men") or the end (like "pen" versus "pens"). If you just replaced the first letter immediately, you wouldn't recognize the word as easily. Because of this, we have two-letter combinations to mean a different sound. "Dog" is *madra,* "my" is *mo,* but "my dog" is *mo mhadra,* with *mh* sounding like *w.* This interesting feature takes a little getting used to, but it is much more consistent than English spelling and pronunciation rules, and it gives the language a wonderful sound and melody.

The fact that the original letter remains, despite the change in sound, also means that you can look up that word in a dictionary. For example, with *i gcrann* for "in a tree"—the *c* is silent but essential for recognizing the original word, *crann,* in case you want to look it up. I see this as a great helping feature for learners. All good courses will cover the phonetic rules in just a short lesson or two.

Learning new vocabulary, despite less familiar words, is very straightforward. You start to recognize word beginnings and ends and can even deduce the meanings of new words. "Astronomy" is *réalteolaíocht* (*réalta* = "star," *eolas* = "knowledge" or "information," *íocht* = the suffix [such as -y, -ity, etc.]; or more generally, the second part, *eolaíocht* = "science," so "star science"). And then sometimes we just separate the words in an easy way. "Exit" is simply *bealach amach* ("way out").

For much more about Irish, including videos and many resources, see fi3m.com/irish.

Sign Language

One of my favorite languages is American Sign Language. It is indeed different in each country; British Sign Language (BSL) is vastly different, although ASL took a lot of inspiration from French Sign Language (LSF, Langue des Signes Française).

This feels like the most natural language to use, as you express yourself fully with your body—so much so that I find it more efficient to use to express many concepts than spoken or written languages.

One of the best things by far, though, is that after learning the alphabet very well (both recognizing it and practicing doing it yourself), a beginner never needs a dictionary or to refer back to a spoken language. Once you have done this, whenever you come across a sign you don't understand, you simply ask the person you are signing with to finger-spell it for you, and you can do the same, finger-spell a word when you don't know its sign. You will have to do this a lot, at the start, and get used to people finger spelling quickly, but the great thing is that you can stay within sign language as a learner.

When you do learn a new sign, it is almost always intuitively logical. The sign incorporates a position relative to the body or a shape or an action, or it adapts the sign of a letter, which makes its meaning apparent. As such, sometimes you can even guess when you aren't confident, to fill in the gaps.

With some wording changes (you don't *speak* from day one, but *sign* from day one), a lot of what I wrote about already is applicable to learning sign language. Try to spend time with signers, deaf or hard of hearing people, or sign language teachers from the very beginning and get used to using the language for real with them. You don't even have to live near a deaf community (such as Gallaudet University in Washington, DC, or the Texas School for the Deaf in Austin, Texas) because you can learn it via Skype! If anything, video calls over Skype, Google+, your smartphone, or other like systems are ideally suited to ASL because of how visual the language is. Finally, there are countless wonderful video blogs (vlogs) in ASL on YouTube.

For much more on ASL and other sign languages, see fi3m .com/sign.

Other Languages

I hope you are seeing in this book that it's all about getting started with saying something. The purpose of this chapter has been to give you some encouragement in whatever language you may be learning and to show you that you can look at its complex features in a different way, so that you can get into using the language as soon as possible.

There are so many languages, I couldn't possibly cover them all in this chapter, but I hope this sample helps most of you. If the language you are learning is not listed here, don't worry. I have written encouraging summaries, or used guest posts from a speaker of that language to write a summary, and you can find them on fi3m.com/langs, with new ones added regularly.

For more about concepts related to grammar in language learning, grammatical features like cognates, modal verbs, conjugations, and much more related to topics introduced in this chapter, check out fi3m.com/ch–6.

CHAPTER 7

From Fluency to Mastery

Strive toward fluency and beyond by coming back to the academic aspects better suited to this part of the language learning process.

In chapters 5 and 6, I described how to get off to a great start in another language. Once you have momentum, you're off and running. It's not necessarily about having a "perfect" approach, but continuing with a learning strategy that encourages you to improve and helps you make those improvements.

Your own approach may differ from my suggestions, and people, of course, learn in very different ways. In my experience, though, applying the methods of chapter 5 have helped me and many others get into languages and achieve a basic conversational level in a language much more quickly than through almost any other approach.

The first step is the most important one. There's no point discussing *perfecting* your language skills before you have definitely started using them. So many language learning approaches are so hung up on perfection that they simply overlook those first steps, and it's why so many people ultimately get nowhere.

But the truth is it's very hard to reach fluency or beyond in a second language through exposure and usage alone, which I have focused on up to now. It's possible and it does happen that people simply *live* the language and are later almost as good as a native speaker. The problem is that this is a very slow method.

Using the tactics we've learned so far, for instance, the person I'm speaking to will need to adjust to my level, speak slowly and clearly, and limit the kinds of things he or she can talk to me about. I will naturally misspeak, but I can indeed talk spontaneously with the person even within these limitations.

But don't let this hold you back, because it's time to move on! We can now strive toward B2 fluency and onward to C2 mastery, including improving our writing and reading skills.

Always Look for Ways to Improve

We have already seen how plateaus can hold us back and how mini-missions can help us overcome them. But it's easy to forget these when we finally reach a stage where we can communicate in a language.

After working so hard to get here, it's almost too easy to get lazy and decide that what we have now is good enough. This is why so many people reach a certain level and stay there indefi-

nitely; they've already put so much hard work in and they feel
they deserve to reap the benefits of all that work.

It can be so tempting to stop learning and just use the language as you can now, because it's "good enough," especially if
you can perform most of your essential social and other basic
interactions in that language. But if you are still conducting your
most complex discussions in your native language, it's important to remind yourself that your work is not done; in fact, the
most fun part of all lies ahead!

Having reached that C2 (mastery) level myself, I can confirm
that the extra work is so worth it! Being able to do anything that
you could possibly want in the target language, including
working in it, having very complex discussions in it, and so
much more, is a whole world apart from being able to have
conversations with a patient speaker.

To reach these upper levels, you have to continue to eliminate plateaus, seriously examine what your biggest problems
are right now, and solve them.

When I was starting to get comfortable with my A2 Mandarin, for instance, and started to set my sights on B1 and beyond,
I found that I could meet up with someone in person and chat
about basic things pretty well. But I was relying a bit too much
on context and, especially, visual cues. When I realized this,
my next step—trying to have more conversations on Skype *with
the video turned off*—seemed the best way to force me to focus
on the words themselves. When I did this for the first time,
even though I had already been learning Mandarin intensively

for a couple of months, I felt like I was starting over from scratch again due to how challenging it was, and my head actually hurt from having to think so much during the session.

It wasn't fun (at first), but thanks to focusing on a problem that I knew I had, I pushed my level up. And now my conversations are better both in person and via Skype. I've pushed my understanding level up several notches and forced myself to recognize many more words than I could with my temporary fix of extrapolating what they were *likely* to mean, which is what I did to help me get through earlier stages.

Traditional Learning Suddenly Becomes Useful

It's very hard to give a precise road map of what to fix, because we each run into different problems due to our varied focuses, learning strategies, passions, language choices, and personal challenges. Some of these are like the one I suggested previously with my Mandarin, which required some lateral thinking to see the best way to solve it.

But at the end of the day, many of these problems can be what I'd call *content problems*—problems with how the language itself operates (how to conjugate verbs, structure sentences, acquire vocabulary, and so on), as opposed to confidence issues or a lack of familiarity, which are actually much bigger problems most of the time for beginners.

The good news with content issues is that the majority of language learning material out there focuses specifically just on content problems. Almost every single language learning course is all about how a language works, with technical explanations of why grammar works the way it does, how words are formed, the rules of how a letter is pronounced differently in different words, and so on.

I think it's a mistake to focus just on pure content issues for the start of your language learning project, especially the way they are presented in most courses; they're simply too boring, and they're not immediately relevant, because there are so many rules to cover that you feel like it will take years to get through them.

But if you first focus on *communication*, by patching words and sentences together as best as you can, then you get a true sense of how a language works and the start of an intuition for how to use it.

That's why, for me, saying *something* is my priority until I reach the basic conversation level, even if I am speaking Tarzan-esque in that language. To hell with speaking perfectly— mistakes help communication flow! But once you have that basic flow, it's time to go to those book courses to start to get some solid footing in communicating formally in the language.

Dealing with Grammar

One of my favorite aphorisms is that grammar is like a really powerful pharmaceutical: it's helpful in small doses but fatal when overprescribed.

And indeed, the most intimidating aspects of learning languages for so many people is all that *grammar*. I was trying to get my head around German in school, and to this day I only remember the language as consisting of nothing more than mindboggling *der, die, das* tables; accusative, dative, and nominative adjective-ending lists; and many other things that seemed way too robotic to inspire me to communicate with people.

Many years later, I rebooted my project to learn German using the strategies in chapter 5 and progressed much more quickly to make wonderful friends through German. But when I reached a certain level, where pure practice couldn't carry me further very fast, it was time to turn back to those grammar books, and something very curious happened.

I found it incredibly interesting.

The problem with learning grammar at the start of our language projects, or when we are not used to truly communicating in the language at some level, is that we have nothing to attach all these boring rules to. It's an inhuman list of rules that can put us off a language before we get started. But after we have learned some of this language, heard it used in real life, tried to communicate in it, and been exposed to lots of real material and genuinely tried to understand it, then we have some *meat* to attach to this supportive skeleton.

When you already know a little of that language and then come across a grammar rule, rather than see some dull explanation you'll quickly forget, your reaction may actually be "So *that's* why they say it that way!" It's almost like putting in the missing piece of a huge puzzle or focusing a camera. That missing piece is meaningless without the other pieces around it, and that focus isn't worth improving if you aren't looking at something specific with your camera.

This is why I suggest only learning grammar in small chunks for the absolute basics, or going through courses that are much more conversation focused and sprinkle a little grammar into it in interesting ways. For most language learners, going for pure grammar or taking grammar-focused courses at the start is a mistake.

But when you *do* speak the language fairly well, then you can actually turn grammar lessons into your mini-mission.

This approach to studying grammar—applying it to what I know, making sure that I can start to form correct sentences, using it to help me understand replies in the context of what each part of a sentence is—ultimately allows me to bring my level up a notch. Thanks to this, I have been able to bring my conversational B1 level up to a fluent B2 many times, because I can express myself much better and understand what is being said to me in ways that purely learning words and phrases can't help with.

With continued studying, and of course *plenty of practice*— especially focused on the grammar points you have studied—you will soon absorb what you need. There will always be something left to learn, but I find that with most (European) languages, the bulk of the grammar is something that brings you up to a good fluent level. This is why I study as much grammar and do as many book-assigned exercises as I need to until I am sure I understand what I learned (with teachers or by running some of my exercises in traditional courses past native speakers, if possible), since this is a major part of my strategy to improve from my basic conversational level.

More Complex Discussions

While your ability to express yourself and understand others will definitely improve when you move from level B1 to B2, I find that the actual content of the conversations can be somewhat similar, depending on how you use the language, of course.

In my case, in both levels I am able to participate in social situations; but in the first one, I require people to speak to me slowly and adjust the way they speak for my benefit. At this level, I won't understand if they speak naturally to their friends, so I can't participate in group discussions.

When I reach B2, people can relax around me and talk faster, and they don't have to "dumb down" the conversation for my benefit. But despite this, I'm still getting to know them better through asking what they do for a living, asking for their back-story and giving mine, making plans, and talking about some-thing topical but lighthearted that people might discuss in a social situation. Certainly a much more varied set than what I was doing in level B1, but it's still friendly chatting.

Once again, I'm tempted to stop here, because ultimately this will be what I'd do the majority of the time in my language: use it to get to know people and have straightforward chats socially, especially as I travel and get to know new people. With a level B2, you can effectively participate in the majority of conversations you may end up having.

But if anyone asks me for my political or philosophical opinions or asks me to defend a point of view or something more complex, I'm stumped, unable to offer my thoughts in a complex way.

That's why, when it's time to push on to the next level, I force myself to have these conversations, so I have no choice but to learn how to express myself when they happen. Whether I'm getting spoken lessons or doing an exchange or simply hanging out with friends, I try to move away from superficial chats about how things are in general and steer the conversation toward very complex discussions.

I defend my philosophical arguments for being an atheist, talk about the vast differences in wealth and poverty I've seen in my travels, try to provide a scientific or technical explanation for how something works based on my engineering and online media experience, ponder the true meaning of happiness from a purely psychological point of view—things that I happen to be passionate about and enjoy discussing.

It can be as frustrating to have these conversations when you are still stuck at level B2 as it is to try to have a simple conversation when you are just beginning to learn, but as with everything else on this path, you need practice to drag yourself up a level or two!

If I have a good teacher or language-exchange partner, we decide on a topic and try to argue points of view. In my best languages, I've tried to go a step further and even argue *against* something I actually believe in so that I'm forced to use different arguments and try to expand on my ability to express a point of view. This would, of course, be during a formal learning session, rather than something I'd do in a casual discussion.

These conversations pressure me to use more complex terminology and vocabulary related to the argument itself or related turns of phrase, such as "that may be true, however . . ." or "I think you're dancing around the real issue," which you might use in such complex discussions. This in turn sends me back to my vocabulary studies and even to my grammar book for certain trickier sentence forms. Once again, studying is used in between sessions of genuinely speaking the language.

If you are in the country itself, you can, of course, join debate or discussion groups or go to events that would push you up a level. Otherwise, you can find online forums to participate in that focus on complex topics or get a private teacher to help you with such specific topics of discussion.

Input: Working Toward Mastery Through Movies and Books

In this book, you will notice that I have prioritized interacting with those who speak the target language; studying is almost an afterthought. This is different from many other approaches, which tend to be more *input* focused; that is to say, the work is to absorb the language in less interactive ways, such as reading, watching TV and movies, and listening to the radio.

The reason for this is because my priority is to communicate *live* in the language, so I need to practice that interactive communication first, much more than I need to be able to read or understand movies well. Being able to understand a TV show or read a newspaper simply doesn't help me as effectively when traveling in a country or socializing with people as much as spoken practice does.

But there is a point when I tend to shift my focus toward more of these input methods, using material that isn't interactive. I usually turn to input methods when I'm trying to jump from fluency to mastery. Before I have learned enough words in interactive conversations, materials I tend to enjoy in English would be too complex for me in the target language to enjoy on a similar level. For instance, I can't enjoy comedy shows (except for slapstick or very simple jokes) in a language as a beginner, so I generally avoid them until I reach fluency. Then I dive into everything I would tend to enjoy in English, but in my target language.

I remember trying to watch a comedy TV show in Spain as a beginning learner: *Aquí No Hay Quien Viva*, about the antics apartment-block neighbors get up to. The jokes and level of speech was just too far beyond me. I tried to watch it for "practice," but I really felt that I had learned nothing after the hour. Since it wasn't interactive, the speakers weren't slowing down a little for my benefit, as those I'd speak to directly would.

Then again, after reaching C2 (mastery) level in Spanish, I started watching the same show (technically rebranded and now called *La Que se Avecina*), and there are many moments when I am almost crying in laughter. It's one of my favorite shows, and I can appreciate it now that I brought my level up enough to be able to truly enjoy it. What I could have done, though, was use this or a similar show when I was at level B2 and study it intentionally to try to bring my level up.

I also read newspapers, listen to radio debates, and enjoy novels in my stronger languages to bring my levels toward mastery. Doing these at first is quite challenging at a B2 level of fluency, where I still need to refer to a dictionary, stop and think for a moment to understand what I heard, or look up complex sentences. It definitely pushes me to my limits, and after a complex session of listening or reading, I can feel exhausted if I have tried very hard to keep up, but I'll be that much better for it next time!

Find as much of this as you can to bring your level up toward mastery. I wouldn't recommend jumping into complex themes as a beginner, though. It's just too complicated for you to even appreciate on a small level. This kind of frustration is a major contributor to why so many learners give up; they try to process native material just after starting, see that it's too hard, and give up entirely. When you instead try to speak to people, it's a lot easier to get eased into it and control the direction the conversation goes, so you can feel some sense of achievement even as a beginner.

If your focus is much more reading- and listening-based than spoken, though, you can—and will—find great ways to get into appreciating input, even as a beginner. Simpler content, or that which you are familiar with in some way, can be a huge boost.

I sometimes watched *The Simpsons* while trying to learn Spanish. Because I had already seen every episode in English and pretty much knew what each character was saying, I could learn new Spanish words and understand them as they were being said, which gave me a tremendous boost of confidence. Others have read comic books or manga in their target language, and the images certainly provide tons of context to fill in the gaps.

Input can be a huge help when you know that it's appropriate to your level or just above it. But hearing a constant stream of noise or needing to look up every single word in a dictionary can be terribly frustrating. It's also an inefficient learning experience. Then again, as I've said elsewhere in the book, there is no one way to learn a language, and many have told me that they have successfully brought their level up through lots of pure input. The catch is that it definitely takes much more time to interact with a language when you delay speaking with a pure-input approach. This is ultimately why it takes years for so many people to reach a conversational level, when others do it in a few months. The former are simply not practicing conversations enough for that aspect of their language skills to improve.

Efficient input works only when you give it your full attention. I thought that simply having the radio on in German for many hours every day would help me learn the language through some kind of osmosis, that it would naturally seep in. But language doesn't work that way. Expecting to learn a language while doing something else is lazy and counterproductive. *Focus is the key.*

If you are listening to audio, don't do something else at the same time; instead, take notes to make sure you are following what you're hearing, or try to repeat it over to yourself, making sure you understand each word. The less attention you give to it, the less efficiently you will learn. You could spend ten hours listening to audio while you are jogging and thinking about something else, but you would learn as much as if you had simply listened to a single hour while pausing and thinking about what was being said with your full focus. Don't multitask language learning!

When I'm jogging or driving, I review past audio I have already focused on while sitting down and in study mode, or alternatively, I listen to audio I am going to go back over later, now that I've heard it all through a single time without pauses. I use the multitasking period as prep time rather than counting it as study time.

Taking an Exam to Force Your Level up a Notch

In my opinion, the fastest path to reaching mastery in a language is the opposite of what many of us typically do. We tend to have structured academic lessons at the start, followed by lots of exposure later on when we feel "ready" to naturally progress toward perfection.

If you follow the advice in the previous chapters, you will of course be getting all that exposure and practice in your early stages and you won't make it about exams and completing chapters of language learning books.

But this kind of structure can be precisely what we need in later stages. That's why I recommend you consider aiming to take an officially accredited examination for your language that is one level higher than where you feel you are now, which will force you to work up to that level. Find an exam appropriate to your language and see if the exam date set for the level above your current one is within a realistic time frame for you to attempt to take and pass it. Then you will typically find past examples and study materials, and you can focus on becoming more familiar with how the exam works for your next desired level.

People who enjoy the technical aspects of language learning may even get great benefits out of taking exams in the earlier stages. I know many successful language learners who pace themselves by taking each level—A1, A2, B1, B2, and upward—every few months. This can be a great way to be absolutely sure of your level, but I find that due to the academic nature of the tests, I personally get more benefit out of taking exams only in levels B2, C1, or C2, at the levels where a more academic approach is more beneficial to my language learning strategy.

A looming deadline forces you to do things you may avoid in the earlier stages, such as sticking to the kind of material you may not otherwise have the patience for.

I have prepared to take three C2 examinations—one in Spanish, which I passed safely; one in German, which I failed by a hair; and one in Italian, which I prepared for but didn't take due to travel issues. In each case, my otherwise fluent level was forced up several notches. I have also met up with teachers to review written exercises I've done. We discuss complex themes so I can expand my vocabulary and turns of phrase, and they assign me readings that I will be tested on in the next lesson.

There *are* people who are structured enough to do this themselves throughout their learning experiences, but I think most people prefer to use the language in ways more immediately relevant to them. They require a little guidance to get them to do exercises or read about and discuss topics they might not otherwise. Without this extra nudge, most of us would only expand our language abilities in topics we find interesting, but in the real world, we have to use our language for more than just this.

This exam structure helps us bring our levels up, and I think it definitely has its place. It should just be applied less at the start and more near to the end, when we have the meat of a language and require refining. It can give us the sophistication and command we require to use the language in as many situations as possible.

Writing, Reading, and Listening?

Formal language education generally divides language learning into four aspects: writing, reading, listening, and speaking. One controversial aspect of my advice is that I say we should focus much less on writing and reading in the early stages, and even on listening (when it is done alone with prerecorded audio, since we are going to improve our skills here by default in conversations). This is not applicable to everyone, but I feel that for most of us a language is several times more relevant when we are speaking to another person than during any of the other options. Rather than devoting 25 percent of our energy to each of the four aspects, I think it's wiser for beginners—especially those who want to travel to a country and interact with people or use the language with friends and family—to devote most of their energy to improving spoken skills, which in turn naturally improves listening skills.

I would devote just 10 to 20 percent of my time to reading and (noninteractive) listening in my initial A1/A2 beginner stages of language learning. For writing, as a beginning learner I am simply not going to write letters or complex messages, but I do write short text messages on my phone.

This is another reason why I feel you can reach spoken level B2 in a few months; you can genuinely have fluent conversations at this level, without necessarily having written or other language skills. You can refine these skills separately and will do so more quickly having reached a conversational level above this. My spoken skills ultimately lift my other skills up when I work on them, and much faster than if I were working on all aspects at the same time.

On the other hand, when I'm securely within level B2 and ready to advance through C1 and on to C2, the tables turn. I then spend only 10 to 20 percent of my time in conversation and (thanks to motivation from signing up for an exam, as I explained previously) divide the rest of my time between *reading* complex texts, *writing* assignments that will get corrected by a native teacher or a motivated friend, and *listening* to complex audio interviews or watching video discussions that I have to test myself on afterward.

If your focus is very different from mine and your passion lies in being able to follow movies in your target language, adjust this and get into movies earlier in your language learning journey. But thanks to my spoken focus, I have had so much practice by the time I reach B2, the only thing really stopping me from progressing is a lack of vocabulary and experience with the subject matter. I've met others at my same general level, with vastly superior writing, reading, and listening skills, but who are way less confident and versatile in spoken situations because of the lack of practice. I can bluff my way through even complex conversations thanks to this confidence from all the practice. This type of exposure to conversations should never be underestimated.

Of course, the ultimate goal when you want to advance toward mastery is not to rely on bluffing at all but to truly understand.

Thinking in the Language

Thinking in the language for most people refers to your inner dialogue, and I force myself to do this *from the start*.

If I'm out of milk, say, rather than think (in English) *Damn! No more milk. Looks like I'll have to go to the store,* I force myself to have this same inner dialogue in the language I'm learning. If I don't know a word, I need to look it up, because my inner dialogue typically follows the kind of vocabulary I would use and the conversations I would have casually with friends. As mentioned previously, if I don't know the words, then I'll still have that dialogue, just with simpler choices and bad grammar, like *Oh no! No milk. I must go store!*

I think this is an essential part of advancing in a language, because a major crutch we rely on in the beginning stages is constantly thinking through translations. We form a sentence in our mind *in English* and then try to search our minds, word by word, for how to say it in our target language. Not only does this slow us down, but our native tongue also influences our word order and grammar.

This is why a lot of successful language learners try to talk to themselves as much as they can, presuming they can't meet up with native speakers (which I hope I have shown in chapter 4 is much less of an issue nowadays). But even if you *can* talk to people, try to fill your alone time with some thinking (aloud or to yourself) in the language. When I walk along a street and see a dog or a hat or a fast bus or an advertisement or a traffic light or anything else, I try to have my inner dialogue comment on that, or I see if I know the word for that thing or can understand a word I see. I'll naturally come across something I don't know the word for and I will force myself to think of alternative ways to describe it, or I'll take out a pocket dictionary or app and look it up.

You can learn in every moment by getting inspired by your surroundings. Thinking in the language is a decision you make, not something that magically happens. Force yourself to think in the language whenever you might otherwise think via your mother tongue and you will speed the language learning process.

Training your inner dialogue means that, in later learning stages, you skip the slow process of translating what you want to say and just say *it* in the language, because you are not only thinking in that language but it is now flowing out of you naturally and immediately. Thanks to forcing myself to think in a language and ask myself questions in that language, I don't translate my Spanish, French, and other languages anymore. I hear a word and just understand it. I want to say a word and just say it. No long sidetracking via English.

There's a Time for Academics

师傅领进门，修行在个人

Shī fu lǐng jìn mén, xiū xíng zài gè rén.

Teachers open the door. You enter by yourself.

—CHINESE PROVERB

While I am trying to make people as independent as possible in their language learning adventures, when you reach a certain stage there are definitely advantages to going back to academic material, examinations, grammar lessons, and such. I still don't think their right place is at the very start of the language learning journey, but they can certainly help you at the right time in the journey.

Just remember that this material is there for a purpose: to improve your language skills. This is not the same as "teaching" you a language. You can never truly be *taught* a language. But you can use teachers, exams, grammar books, and exercises to help you solve problems when you are at a stage to charge on toward mastery.

For more information about CEFRL examinations and any alternatives for non-European languages, as well as a more detailed explanation of what each of the various levels means, visit fi3m.com/cefrl.

For a more detailed explanation of the ideas introduced in this chapter, resources for improving your writing, reading, and listening skills, and how to combine traditional learning approaches with an independent learning approach, see the videos and links at fi3m.com/ch-7.

CHAPTER 8

How to Get Mistaken for a Native Speaker

It's time to go beyond fluency by adapting to the local culture, until a stranger mistakes you for a native!

By applying what I've discussed about academic courses, grammatical exercises, and taking exams, I have managed to reach a genuine C2 level (mastery) several times. This means I can effectively do absolutely everything in that language that I can in English, including my work as an engineer and discussions on complex topics.

But I may still have an accent, and people still know I'm a foreigner. This is not something that is brought up on the CEFRL language scale, because having an accent doesn't affect what you can actually do in the language. There isn't a C3 level—which might be a C2 but without an accent—and with good reason.

Does an Accent Make You Seem Native?

I think people should examine *why* they want to reduce their accents. The benefits of blending in with people from another country are not just about having no accent, but about being confused for a native speaker. These are two very different worlds.

I'll discuss accent reduction shortly, but even if you have an accent, you can still get confused for a native speaker. And being confused for a native speaker isn't just about *sounding* like one, but *acting* like one.

I go out of my way to emulate the clothing sense, body language, distance between speakers, facial expressions, the topics I discuss, and all things related to what native speakers would do, rather than just how they would say something. This requires paying attention to customs, looking at what people are doing, and picking up on these things.

While this is, of course, much harder to do when you are in a place where skin color makes you stand out, I don't think you should give up hope. Many countries are much more multiethnic than you may think, and it is easier to blend in. Even in an extreme case, like China, which has a very tiny amount of non-Asian immigration, people have confused me for an English teacher who has lived in China for years, based on a combination of my speaking Mandarin and standing out less by *acting* more Chinese.

Walk Like an Egyptian

For instance, when I arrived in Egypt with the beginnings of B1 level spoken Arabic, I found that people would still talk to me in English, *before I even said anything*. So improving my Arabic clearly wasn't the issue here. Many might say that my skin color makes it impossible to blend in, but this isn't entirely true; it's not about blending in perfectly, but standing out less. Major cities like Cairo actually do have white Egyptians, but the trick is to not look like a white tourist.

So I took the time to sit down at a café where many people were passing by and, with a notepad, really paid attention to what was different between them and me from a purely visual perspective. I noticed that Egyptian males around my age (at least in Cairo) tended to have mustaches and they definitely didn't wear the kind of lightweight clothes I preferred in that hot weather, but instead wore sweaters, long pants, and dark shoes. They also walked pretty confidently and were much more likely to be talking on their cell phones while crossing a busy street with high-speed traffic coming at them. I also noticed they were less likely to wear hats.

I got rid of my cap, started wearing a sweater over my T-shirt, and as much as I really wanted to wear my comfortable bright-yellow sneakers, I put on cheap, dull, black shoes I found in a local market instead. I also let a mustache grow out and maintained some stubble to look more like Egyptian men my own age.

The way people first treated me after this transformation was incredible! Even though I am definitely Irish and as white as you'd expect any Irish guy to be, people always started speaking *Arabic* to me when I entered a store, including in highly touristed areas where they spoke very good English, or they would continue in Arabic after I asked a question. Something about my outward appearance helped keep the conversation in the right language.

I am convinced that this outward appearance and body language are as essential as the things I mentioned in the previous chapter when reasoning why some locals may feel inclined to switch back to English. When you look like a tourist, there is a certain subconscious thought process screaming at them to speak English with you, even if you are audibly doing great in their language.

Blending in Beyond Spoken Abilities

Keeping all this in mind, I have found that in Brazil I should swing my arms behind my back while I walk and try to make physical contact while speaking (for instance, putting my hand on someone's shoulder while I talk to the person, whether male or female). In France, I sit with my legs crossed, as I have noticed men tend to do that more frequently there. When in Asian countries, I take someone's business card or hand out mine or hand over cash with both hands in a slow and deliberate gesture. In many countries, when out in a bar and saying the local equivalent of "cheers," I maintain eye contact while saying it. I also always check how I use my arms; too much gesturing in some countries can make people feel like you are a maniac likely to knock something over, but too little in others can make you seem stiff and inexpressive.

I can spot Americans instantly, because they tend to smile a bit too much (in many countries, smiles are not used to break the ice or ease the tension, like in the States, but only when you are genuinely happy; and as such, smiles come across as insincere when overused) and because of a "personal bubble" of distance Americans and English-speaking Canadians tend to keep between themselves and other people while speaking.

Of course, it's very easy to point out exceptions to these rules; you can't generalize about hundreds of millions of people. But there are certain traits that each culture is likely to have, and you can find these by observation or time spent with natives. Keep this in mind and you will more likely have the people you meet thinking you are a native—at least visually. Even if you have the most convincing accent in the world, if you are breaking too many visual rules, it's very unlikely you will get confused for a native speaker.

These changes will also ensure the other person is more comfortable and eager to keep talking to you, because intruding into someone's personal space (such as what westerners may do from an Asian perspective), keeping at too much of a distance (such as northern Europeans and North Americans do in Latin countries), wearing "weird" clothes, or having unexpected facial expressions and body language sends an unspoken message to that person that you don't respect him or her in some way. This can be why a conversation ends abruptly, regardless of your spoken level.

Here are a few things to observe about native speakers (by watching television or relating in person), especially those who are the same gender and age as you:

- What clothes do they typically wear?

- What facial expressions do they have as they speak?

- What distance are they from other speakers?

- What are they doing with their hands?

- How do they handle personal grooming and what hairstyles do they have?

- How and how fast do they walk?

- What postures do they have when standing or sitting?

- How much eye contact do they make?

- What other unique features that make them different from you could you potentially emulate?

Rolling Your R

After outward appearance and general way of acting, the next obvious reason that people will know you are a foreigner is your accent.

The first component of accent reduction is to look at the individual sounds you can't create right now. Even the most basic language courses will cover in an early lesson the differences between your native tongue and the target language.

Prioritize fixing these to be as close to the real sounds as early as possible, because there are always a tiny number of sounds you need to learn, and if you do this right, you can have the beginnings of a much improved accent as you are pronouncing basic terms. Because there are just half a dozen or so new sounds you need to learn how to produce, focus on them as early as the first week, if you can. You don't have to say these new sounds perfectly, but if you get them close enough, and quickly enough, you'll find it a lot easier to make them more precise with time than if you had used English equivalents.

Some of these are incredibly easy to mimic quickly. For instance, the German ü and the French u can both be approximated surprisingly well by rounding your lips as if you are going to say an *oo* sound but then actually say an *ee* sound. It's more complicated than this, but even this approximation can be worth practicing your very first day so that you are close to the actual sound.

Another one that is much easier to do than people believe is the *alveolar flap*—the r (between two vowels, like in *caro*) that appears in many languages, such as Spanish, Portuguese, Italian, Slavic languages, and many more. What so many people don't realize is that they can already approximate this sound, even if they can only speak English. Do *not* try to change your English r to a flapped or rolled one, because this is far too different. You may as well try to learn how to say the letter *m* by starting with a *k* sound, in terms of how well connected they are!

No, in fact, we produce something incredibly similar (at least in American English) when we say the word "butter." Not that *r* at the end, but that *tt* sound in the middle! Say it now *quickly* in a sentence, so you are less focused on forcing an unnatural pronunciation, and rather than an explosive *t* sound, like in "time," you have a flap of the tongue. Now change that *b* to a *c* and say "cutter" the same way. Then change the *er* sound to an *o* sound and say it a few times, watching that you aren't saying a *t* sound but maintaining the flap sound. Finally, open your mouth wider to change the *u* sound to an *a* and you have that word *caro* (which means "expensive" in Spanish and Portuguese).

It's certainly weird to get an *r* sound out of what is written as a *t* sound, but this is much closer to what we want in terms of mouth positions. It's also a much better starting point from which to merge into an alveolar flap later, and we temporarily use it to make sure that what we are saying is clearer to a native ear than a very English barking *r*.

Another way to approximate the alveolar flap is to say *la,* followed by *da,* and do so very quickly. Try saying "la, da, la, da, la, da," and so on. You will notice that you keep moving your tongue forward and backward. Now try to stop it somewhere halfway. It's easier than you think!

There are a host of other sounds, which I won't cover here, but look them up on YouTube, where they are explained very well. In many segments, a native will explain how a sound works and give suggestions for how to say it. This helps much more than reading an explanation, because you can hear how it should sound and mimic it along with the video. This way you can get a pretty good command of those few sounds that are different from your mother tongue.

When you take on the challenge of trying to sound more like a native, focus on pronunciation and sit down with a native speaker (in person or during an online call) who can tell you precisely why you are pronouncing something incorrectly. If you do this, I would highly recommend that you ask the native speaker to mimic how *you* are saying it followed by how it *should* be said. It's a little embarrassing to feel like someone is mocking your bad sound, but this has helped me notice the real difference much more quickly.

I remember that I spent several hours trying to roll my *r*, and over several days I tried to mimic a purring cat while relaxing my tongue and blowing air over it. Tougher sounds like this, which are nothing like what you have in your native language, can take some getting used to, but practice and feedback from natives can help you create them. There is nothing stopping you from genuinely learning them. The idea that your tongue doesn't have the muscles—or other such excuses—is nothing but ridiculous.

This practice is important to both getting the approximation of a new sound and aspiring to sound like a native while you tweak those lingering minor mistakes.

Singing Your Accent Away

Having a convincing accent is, of course, what most of us consider a crucial factor in being confused for a native speaker. I think this only works when combined not just with having an overall native-like appearance, but also with what you're saying. It's not just *how* you say something but *what* you say.

Even if you use grammatically perfect sentences and do so with a pristine accent, and even if you outwardly look like a native, if you say things that are not generally said in that country, you will stand out like a sore thumb.

For instance, the English phrase "go to bed" is grammatically incorrect if you consider it compared to going anywhere else, which requires an article (go to *the* kitchen, go to *a* bathroom) or a possessive (go to *my* car). Despite this, the phrase is "go to bed." Exposure to natives and imitating and repeating what they say will give you real phrases.

This is how I prefer to work on improving my accent: by saying several words that are genuinely uttered by a native, learning sentence blocks, and processing my flash cards not as individual words but as new words in example sentences, which give them better context than learning a single translation from English.

There are sounds we create by combining words, and we can't get these from learning the sounds of individual words too well. While "my" may theoretically be pronounced to rhyme with "buy," when said as one word or when speaking slowly, many native English speakers alter this a bit and say "ma" when speaking quickly (in Ireland we even go so far as to say it as "mee"). Vowel sounds naturally get cut shorter and some consonants disappear altogether in English.

These are not described accurately in slowly enunciated audiotapes, which is why I tend to take a native recording, such as a podcast or a TV show, replay a segment, and try to mimic it precisely as well as I can. For instance, many Spanish speakers (depending on which country and region) don't pronounce the *d* in words with *ado* in them; when spoken quickly and naturally, something like *pescado* becomes *pescao*. While this may not be "proper" Spanish, it is how many people speak and should be emulated if you are aiming to mimic the accent of a native—in much the same way "I dunno" is often how we say "I don't know" in English.

For some people, focusing on repeating native-recorded phrases and attempting to reproduce them is all they need. Many language learners get great mileage out of *sentence drilling*, and they do so only with sentences that have been genuinely uttered by natives, rather than translations of what they might say.

For me, this can get boring, so since I am quite musical, I have found that singing to mimic real songs in the language can be a huge help and a good break from repeating phrases. When people sing, they also pronounce the words naturally and quickly (depending on the song or singer).

But rather than do this alone, I have gone back to taking private lessons. Only this time, instead of hiring a language teacher (language teachers are typically not qualified to help with accent reduction; they focus more on language content in terms of vocabulary, grammar, expressions, and the like), I hire a singing or music teacher! I have also had success with voice trainers who specialize in helping radio broadcasters sound more professional in their native tongues. I've even gone to speech therapists—once again, those who work with native speakers aiming to improve their pronunciation. The thing about a singing teacher, a voice trainer, and a speech therapist is that, unlike language teachers, they are very familiar with enunciation, pauses, mouth and tongue positions, rhythm, tonality, and much more.

When I tried to get by as a native Brazilian Portuguese speaker, my Carioca music teacher helped me with singing lyrics to popular Brazilian songs after we read them aloud first. One of her criticisms of my early attempts was that we English speakers . . . tend . . . to separate . . . our words . . . too much . . . as we . . . speak. In Portuguese, words flow together while your intonation goes up and down, and this helps you separate words in your mind better than strict pauses. After I was able to repeat the phrases she gave me to her satisfaction, hearing other foreigners speaking Portuguese and *not* doing it made me immediately think that they sounded like robots with their individual word separations, in comparison to how Portuguese should be spoken.

My music teacher helped me appreciate this and other "musicality" aspects of Portuguese that are applicable even, and especially, when spoken. Singing it helped emphasize the differences even more. It was very hard to push myself to try to sing like a native, and I wasn't completely successful, but in aiming toward something as hard as that, I pushed my *spoken* abilities up several notches and had much more convincing Portuguese pronunciation because of it.

There are even accent trainers who specifically help second-language learners. I like how Idahosa (Mimicmethod.com) does it by taking recordings of his students. He then plays them back to the students, highlighting the particular sounds that betray them as foreigners, and plays them beside the native examples for comparison. If you have a native friend online who you think can help you with precisely recorded phrases, you can practice consistently, then upload it to SoundCloud.com (an audio equivalent of YouTube), and comments can be made at the precise point in the audio where your pronunciation requires a change.

Pronunciation or Intonation?

At first glance, it can seem that the differences between a native accent and a foreign accent are all in the pronunciation, but intonation takes a much more critical role. When I had the chance to chat with a very interesting Italian polyglot, Luca Lampariello, this was made very clear.

Luca can speak a large number of languages and was studying to be an interpreter when I met him, but what really struck me as the most impressive thing about him is that he has almost no noticeable accent in several of his learned languages. When I first heard him speak English, I would have thought he was American, if it weren't for his YouTube channel being called "poliglotta80" (the Italian word for "polyglot"). Natives of other languages, such as German and Spanish, have confirmed that he is incredibly convincing in these languages too.

But he did not grow up speaking these languages. When I asked him about improving pronunciation to have a more convincing accent, he made sure the conversation quickly focused on intonation.

He considers intonation to be like the network that holds a sentence together. The example he gave me was to notice how the word "France" sounds different in a sentence like "France is a beautiful country" versus "I would like to go to France." In the first sentence, when we are not emphasizing particular words, we tend to say the word "France" with its intonation rising upward, but in the second sentence, our intonation tends to go down on the word "France."

As another example, he said, "I want to talk to Mark and John," and if we listen carefully, we hear that we put different tonalities on "Mark" (going up, indicating that the sentence hasn't finished yet or we are giving the first item in a list) and on "John" (the end of factual sentences in English tend to have a downward turn).

Rather than learn these intonation rules individually, Luca recommended that people try to see the general picture of how these rules apply to a language. Appreciating this "network" allows you to step back, see the whole picture, and truly appreciate how a sentence sounds and conveys meaning beyond just its individual words.

He has his own approach for trying to appreciate this visually as well as audibly. You can imagine certain types of sentences that serve a particular purpose (presenting a fact, giving an order, asking a question) following particular prosody patterns (*prosody* is the rhythm, stress, and intonation in speech), then represent these patterns as waves going up and down and try to hum these mini-tunes to yourself before applying them to actual words.

This is also what I do when I am trying to apply these changes to improve my accent; many languages have these kinds of patterns, and I try to learn them outside of saying words. I may bring these up with my accent trainer, as I mentioned just previously.

One issue was pointed out to me recently that would help me improve my French prosody; my musically inclined teacher told me that changes in tones (such as those cued by the commas in English lists) occur less frequently in French. For instance, in English, the middle of sentences don't tend to have rising intonations, such as "What I'm trying to say . . ." which is relatively monotone. In French, on the other hand, the equivalent phrase "Ce que je veux dire . . ." tends to be said with a slight rising tone toward the last word. I had naturally picked this up through lots of exposure and was actually overdoing it when I spoke French, going up at the end of mid-sentence pauses *and* at the end of sentences, where you actually should have a downward intonation. Because of this, my sentences actually sounded more like questions, all the time. When this was explained to me and I made the correction, I was told that it was a dramatic change to what had previously been a very strange sentence rhythm, and it sounded much more naturally French.

Intention

> When a person has an accent, it means
> he can speak one more language than you.
>
> —FERNANDO LAMAS

Don't forget that, while a convincing accent can help you sound like a native speaker, appreciation for a local culture and its customs is what really wins over locals of a country you are visiting. Each time people have seen me try to adapt to these aspects as well as improve my language skills, they have warmed up to me much faster.

Speaking with no accent is not as important as people make it out to be; in many cases, an accent can give you a charm that makes you even more interesting to get to know. This also reminds people that you are still a learner, and they will go easier on you, which helps you enjoy the learning process even more.

With this in mind, when you *are* ready to improve your accent, and you combine it with cultural adjustments, you can even get mistaken for a native speaker. This has happened to me on many occasions, after using a combination of the tips introduced in this chapter, despite the fact that I spent twenty-one years of my life in Ireland before living abroad.

For more thoughts on cultural adjustments and particular accent issues, with suggestions on how to fix them, as well as videos related to intonation and other helpful tricks relevant to this chapter, check out fi3m.com/ch–8.

CHAPTER 9

Hyperpolyglot:
When One Is Just Not Enough

*Take language learning
to the next level. Speak multiple languages
without mixing them up or forgetting the
one(s) you've already mastered.*

Using the tools from previous chapters, you should be able to progress toward fluency and on to that elusive *mastery* level in a single language, and even sound and look convincing as a speaker of that language.

While reaching the B1/B2 spoken level is certainly possible in a matter of months for someone dedicated and putting in considerable hours each day, reaching the mastery stage requires a longer investment to tidy up the mistakes picked up along the way, learn specialized vocabulary, improve reading and writing skills, and absorb the culture intentionally through many sources. Ultimately, after lots of such investment, you'll be as effective in that target language as you are in your native one.

But many people dream of doing so in multiple languages. In this chapter, I'll share the techniques that have worked for me *and* for other people to be able to converse in several foreign languages.

The Catch-22 of Wanting to Be a Polyglot

Not to be confused with a linguist, someone who studies or specializes in linguistics, a polyglot is a person who can speak multiple languages well.

Trying to become a polyglot, however, is a terrible goal! While you can keep this goal at the back of your mind, in my travels, meeting other polyglots and interviewing them about their language learning processes, and in my own experience becoming one, one thing has become blatantly clear across the board: you can only become a polyglot if you are passionate about each language, and not because you want to "collect" a large number of languages.

While it may sound impressive to know Chinese, Arabic, French, and German, if you are not eager to live your life through each language or discover different cultures, fascinating literature, or wonderful and interesting people—also in each individual language—then it's clear you are interested in the wrong things. The same rules apply: if you're not willing to put in the work, your chances of success drop.

That's why you need to pick your languages carefully.

Learning Multiple Languages Simultaneously?

Another aspect of taking on multiple languages, even if you are sure you are passionate about those you are looking at, is the question of whether to jump on all of them at once or take them in succession. While some language learners can take on several new languages at once, most cannot. In fact, for most language learners this is a really bad idea, especially if they don't have any prior experience with other languages.

Someone who already has several languages under his or her belt may be able to take on a couple of new languages simultaneously, but if you have not successfully learned any new languages as an adult already, it's best to focus on just one language at a time. Despite my own experience learning languages, I never try to learn two new languages at once. There is too much of a risk of mixing them up. Grammar rules and vocabulary have a nasty habit of bleeding into each other when you're first trying to get used to them.

While it may seem logical enough to try to learn two languages at the same time for a given period, say French and Spanish, you're actually working against your best language learning interests. You're almost always better off focusing your entire attention on one language and then, once you're comfortable with it, turning your full attention to a second language.

This doesn't mean you have to master one language before moving on to the next one. But you should at least wait until you're fluent in one before taking on another. You should be confident using a language, at a B2 level or above. When I reach this stage in a language, for instance, I find it's then really hard to forget the language, even if I don't practice it for several months or a year.

When I have reached no more than level B1, though, because I am not yet truly comfortable in that language and because it doesn't feel like it's a part of me, it is much more likely to slip away, such that you go down an entire level in a very short time and even forget the basics. Of course, you can still get rusty with lack of practice at a B2 level and above, but within a very short time you can get back to where you used to be.

How Many Languages Can a Person Learn?

The obvious question is, what's the limit? And, since we're on the topic, how many languages do I speak? Whether that number is six, eight, twelve, or fifteen will depend on when you ask me the question and the nature of what "speak" means to you.

The American polyglot Tim Doner agrees with this, and while media mentions of him may list him as speaking twenty languages, he and all other polyglots much prefer to avoid sound bites that work well in newspaper articles; he prefers to give answers that define the levels he may have in each language or list how many he has a mastery level in or how many he can "get by" in, and so on. Generally, a true polyglot is quick to avoid giving simple answers.

For most people, though, such a high number is not necessary or possible, not because they don't have the inherent talent, but because they don't live the kind of travel lifestyle that I do or have the passion for languages other polyglots do, where languages are such a huge part of their daily lives. Learning languages indeed starts to become a full-time job!

But never listen to anyone (including me!) who tells you what your limitations are; I can only speak for my own limitations and suggest that these may apply to other people, as I have done in this book. I have met people busier than I am but more passionate for languages, and they overtake my number of languages at a fluent level or higher. Some would dismiss them as geniuses, but to me it's more a question of passion. In talking to them in person I can feel this passion and appreciate that they are mere mortals, with their own challenges in language learning, but I could see the passion they have as they use and talk about languages. This decides how many languages they can ultimately speak.

I do, however, feel that becoming a polyglot is well within the realm of possibility for mere mortals (of which I count myself!) who can't set aside a vast number of hours each week for learning or maintenance (which was the case for me during the first years of my travels, because I worked full-time in non-language-learning jobs). How many languages you ultimately reach will depend on you, your dedication to and passion for each language, and the time you are willing and able to set aside.

At first, when people hear that I attempt to take on a new language in just three months, they presume this must mean I learn four languages a year. They also think that I should know forty languages because I've been learning foreign languages while traveling for a decade.

There have actually been a lot of languages that I have taken on but decided not to maintain. As a result, my fluency level dropped dramatically. I can still reactivate them and go through the learning stages again, and do so much faster because the language is in there somewhere. But realistically, if you speak to me in that language, I can't engage in the kind of conversation I had when I was focused on that language. Sadly, this has been the case for half of the languages I have taken on.

The reason for this is that when you start to learn as many languages as I have, you reach a limit in the number of hours you can put into them. You have to make some tough decisions. In my case, if I wasn't absolutely inspired to keep living through that language for the rest of my life, I let it go. Some languages, however, have had a much deeper effect on me. I continue to return to and study these languages.

It's always due to pull factors rather than push factors. Irish is important to me as an Irish person. Because Brazil is my favorite country, I'll always speak Portuguese. Spanish represents such an important part of my life, so I'll always try to maintain the language.

No matter how many languages I learn, however, there is a saturation point. I may eventually reach a certain number of languages I maintain and then stick to that number, even if I decide to learn a new language temporarily for travel purposes. There comes a point when you have to accept that taking on a new language would hurt maintaining your current ones too much. You only have a certain finite amount of time and should use it wisely.

Hyperpolyglot: Richard Simcott

Richard Simcott, a well-known British "hyperpolyglot"—a polyglot who speaks six or more languages—has uploaded videos online of himself using sixteen languages in various levels. I met up with Richard to ask him how he learns languages and what polyglots do differently from people learning a single language.

As expected, he agreed with me that there really is no simple answer to this question. He recalled another polyglot we both respect very much, Professor Arguelles, who shares his incredibly intensive approach of getting up early in the morning to write structured and precisely timed reviews of books in many languages. This works excellently for him, as he is passionate about reading languages, but it simply would not work for Richard or me. For the two of us, such a structured approach would destroy our motivation, because we like more spontaneous and random exposures to languages, particularly in spoken contexts.

Richard sees himself as practical. He surrounds himself with the languages he wants to work on by speaking them and consuming media. He says there is no secret or magic formula. The only way to reach fluency, he maintains, is through practice—granted, *a lot* of practice, but this type of pure exposure and time with a language and intentional, focused work toward improvement are key to learning a new language.

When I asked him how many languages he feels someone can practically hope to learn, he said it really depends on how dedicated that person is. "Languages," he said, "are an essential part of my life and work. This has allowed me to put the time into allowing each one to evolve."

While we all imagine a typical impressive polyglot to know a dizzying number of languages, all at a perfect mastery level with no accent, the reality is that polyglots—myself and Richard included—tend to have some languages they are still working to bring up to fluency and a smaller manageable number at the higher levels. Richard says that he has rarely met someone with eight or more languages at a fluent level (as I described fluency earlier). He's also never met someone who has learned a language as an adult who could pass as a native speaker all of the time, even though the person definitely could some of the time. He also doesn't see why someone would want to learn such a huge number of languages, realistically speaking. More numbers may sound "cool," but we never need more than just a few languages in our professional and personal lives.

It's only really those who end up dedicating their work to language learning who reach such high numbers. And more important, those must be willing to dedicate a large portion of their lives to handling such a large number.

In the end, having met many people from the polyglot community, I can see that the number itself becomes less important than the sheer ability to communicate and express yourself in a language you are passionate about.

Not Mixing Up Languages

Now that we've established the ideas behind multilingualism, I can share some techniques that have helped *me* keep track of all the different languages in my head without mixing them up. These are equally applicable whether you have your eye on a large handful of languages or on only two or three.

As I mentioned before, I pick just one language to learn at a time and stick to that until I am very confident in it. When I apply certain techniques to blend in and appreciate the local culture more, I find this seeps into my language skills. Plus, I use body language and a sense of a "personality" with the language to help me keep it separate in my mind. This is more of a psychological tool than a language learning one, but as I learn a language, I make sure I am trying my best to use it as a native would.

For example, in French you have to speak a little in the front of your mouth. This requires you to purse your lips a little to get a more authentic sound. I would learn all my vocabulary this way, sounding it out and trying to do it *à la française*.

Castilian Spanish, on the other hand, tends to be spoken further back in the mouth. This means that a French word like *voiture* simply can't come out of my mouth when I am speaking Spanish, because I have learned this word in a French way and it just *feels weird* to say it another way, even when adding a more Spanish -*o* or -*a* to it. Not only does it not synchronize with the position of my mouth, but the word also doesn't line up with my body language or even the way I *think*.

This mental association helps us naturally compartmentalize languages in our minds, the same way we use certain formal words in work situations and slang ones with our friends. We are in a different mindset in both cases.

Saying a Portuguese word like *falar* with Brazilian body language while trying to *think* like a Brazilian and speak a similar language like Spanish is just not going to happen. Saying anything but *hablar* for "to speak," in Spanish, will sound like an aggressive intrusion to me. Practice and reinforcement mean that the language becomes a part of you, and things like this just sound right—or wrong, as the case may be.

Hearing a word and using it regularly is the best way to make sure you use each language confidently. With time, you will successfully compartmentalize each new language in your mind.

Like Richard, I also have been in environments that have required me to make a switch in a language, such as at international events with people from all around the world. At first, I have stumbled into some weird Franglais, Spanglish, Portuñol,

Denglish, Espaliano, or some other odd mixture of languages, but I can quickly correct myself and remember not to do it again. You simply learn and become good at switching between the languages.

Grammarese

While practice is the key ingredient, and ultimately the rules for learning your nth language are the same as learning your first one, there are certain other tricks of the trade that you can start applying. One of them is that you tend to pick up a side language I like to call *grammarese*.

As I said in chapter 7, starting to learn a language through grammar-heavy materials is something I wholeheartedly recommend *against* for beginning language learners. But once you reach a certain stage, grammar drills and rules can help you improve your skills effectively.

An interesting thing happens after you have gone through grammar rules once or twice; you start to pick up on all the specialized terminology most people are not aware of. I remember when I was training to become an English teacher to help me extend my time in Spain, and I had to relearn the definitions of article, conjugation, adjective, adverb, declension, case, pronoun, determiner, possessive, participle, subjunctive, preposition, and so many other things.

I have come across these terms so many times in so many books by this stage, I feel like I've picked up an extra language, as I can discuss the grammatical features of a language, even though such a thing didn't interest me in the slightest when I first got into all of this.

This is another reason you can learn multiple languages more easily—you don't have to go through learning an oblique language of terminology every time because you have already learned it. This is why I would suggest, when you do get to that B1+ level in your first foreign language, tidying up what you have with some grammar studies. While it may slow you down a little, it's worth the time to truly understand and learn the terminology and presentation of tables, because when you come across a similar explanation in your next language, you will be able to flick through these pages much faster as a result.

When I came to the "notoriously grammatically complex" language of Hungarian, I have to say I didn't find it even the slightest bit intimidating. To me, it seemed perfectly logical and consistent. As I read through heavy grammatical explanations, I didn't see what all the fuss was about. I might even argue against linguistically minded people and tell them that Hungarian's supposed dative and other cases are actually nothing more than agglutinative postposition suffixes that follow very simple vowel harmony rules, and the definite articles don't even have any gender or case declension!

That last sentence would have been nothing but pure gobbledygook to me a few years ago (and may indeed be to many of you reading this), but it now comes naturally. The point is that you start to appreciate a language on a meta-level of how the pieces fit together in this grammatical and linguistic way. You also start to see how language families blend together and evolve apart, and to predict logically how and why a rule should work even before you ever come across it written down, based on your previous experience with other languages.

Learning One Language via Another

The final thing worth mentioning when you have a few languages under your belt is *laddering,* or learning one language via another.

While there is indeed plenty of excellent material to learn various languages through English, I have found that learning through another language I already speak well allows me to learn the new language a little quicker sometimes. Usually I do this through French because I quite like Assimil's language courses, which present languages in an interesting way, and my French is very good.

Learning through other foreign language speakers is another great way to learn a new language through another language. When I first arrived in Italy, for instance, I stayed with an Italian friend, Daniele, whom I had met in Spain. He explained several of my mistakes in Italian *through Spanish,* which really helped me begin to compartmentalize both of these languages as well as appreciate their differences, much more so than I would have by getting the explanations in English.

In fact, when dealing with similar languages, a book explaining how one language works through the other can more effectively point out to you the differences between them. If you then start over with a book explaining the language in English, you will learn many similar rules and vocabulary lists for the similar languages. It's less efficient than learning through a book designed specifically to point out the differences between the two languages.

As such, when I started learning Dutch and kept mixing it up with German, I found that I was able to work much more effectively as soon as I got a book about the Dutch language *written in German.*

When I come across new vocabulary and learn it through the translation of a language I speak well, I start to associate the meaning of a word in my new language with the *concept* of what that word means, rather than a translation through English (or French). This helps me remember it more quickly.

One of the greatest advantages of all, though, is that for about the same amount of work, you learn a new language while effectively maintaining one of your current languages! I always say we should use our languages for what we are passionate about, and if you are passionate about language learning, it only makes sense to use one of your well-established languages for that very purpose.

Live a New Life for Every Language

You live a new life for every new language you speak.
If you know only one language, you live only once.

—CZECH PROVERB

As you have seen in this chapter, I highly recommend you focus on just one language at a time. You may have a goal to take on multiple specific languages, but take your time and make sure you know one very well before you go on to the next one, and you'll be on the road to multilingualism.

Some of the people I mentioned in this chapter and elsewhere in the book have written or made videos extensively about their own learning approaches. In many particular cases they agree with me, and in some cases they branch off and offer alternative advice. This is a good thing! There is no one true way to learn one or many languages, so I would encourage you to investigate other polyglots' language learning advice and see what jives best with you and your goals.

For a list of interesting polyglots and hyperpolyglots, videos of them, and links to their work, and to discover more about their learning approaches and their advice for picking up languages, check out the follow-up to this chapter online at fi3m.com/ch–9.

CHAPTER 10

Free and Cheap
Language Learning 2.0

*Study a new language beyond
spoken practice sessions with invaluable—
and mostly free—resources.*

It's time to discuss the final piece of the puzzle missing from
your language learning artillery—the tools you *need* to study and
learn with.

One of the first things people ask when learning a language
is what courses they should buy. The good news is that you can
actually start learning your language today, right now, for free
or at very little cost. As you have seen in most of this book,
language courses are greatly overshadowed by my advice to use
the language, ideally with another human being—and conversational practice can be found in many instances for free. Even in
this final chapter, I don't want to present some particular course

as able to solve all your problems, but I will discuss other resources for learning a language and improving your skills in that language.

You can get started right away by creating your language learning logs, learning conversational connectors, using good free online dictionaries, finding interesting examinations to take in order to motivate you to push toward a particular level, and implementing spaced repetition learning. And, finally, you can expose yourself to genuine native content in that language.

Cheap Generic Courses vs. Expensive Courses

I get asked all the time my opinion on particular well-marketed language learning courses, especially by Americans overwhelmed by marketing and advertising campaigns. In my experience, the price of a course and its quality, usefulness, and results are not related. In fact, my favorite first resources, which I would buy in a target language, come cheap (between five and thirty dollars) and provide excellent teaching materials.

I've tried Rosetta Stone, for instance. There are some useful bits in it, but far too many aspects of it I didn't like at all. Overall I can't say that a higher price point delivers better results than much more affordable book courses. There are also completely free courses, just as good or better, such as the ones at Duolingo.com.

One thing that is generally effective, if you *do* spend a lot of money, is the purely psychological effect of feeling more pressure to work harder because you've spent so much money. How effective this truly is, is debatable (you can't throw money at all your problems), and I find I get the same kind of pressure from simply being public about my project.

As such, the tools I recommend for learning a language are the following books, which you can get at your local bookshop or on Amazon.com:

For an absolute beginner (phrases and words, with very brief grammatical overview), I suggest a Lonely Planet, Collins, Berlitz, or Assimil phrase book.

Colloquial and Teach Yourself are two basic book courses that provide very good representations of the dialogues tourists are likely to have, and they introduce you to some basic grammar. The presentation is friendly, and they teach what you essentially need to know.

Assimil also creates excellent language learning courses, and I especially like how they indicate the level you are aiming for on the CEFRL scale. As such, I have used Assimil in both the early and later stages of learning, although they have more versatile courses in French, so I use the laddering technique discussed in chapter 9 with this.

Of course, some books, courses, and materials can be better than others depending on the language you are learning. Make sure to see the language-specific summaries at fi3m.com/langs that expand on the language introductions from chapter 6 and go on to mention recommended learning resources.

The Perfect Learning Approach

The courses I listed in the previous section are generic courses in that they provide exactly the same content for vastly different language learners. This is why I recommend that you use them not only as a beginner but also between sessions of doing something more direct with your language.

No course, no matter how convincing its marketing may be, can be the one all-encompassing solution to your language learning problems. This is why I focus on speaking, and I use studying these types of books as my generic improvement for a few hours. But I spend the majority of my hours either speaking the language, fixing particular issues I had in a spoken session or in independent study, or addressing issues I may not find in these courses.

You have to find your own learning style, and that's why I recommend you experiment, but do so in such a way that it is affordable and well directed. A huge problem many language learners have is hoarding language learning material and feeling that they can experiment a little with it all. As mentioned previously, a survey that I ran on my blog clearly showed that successful language learners were more likely to be those who used *less* language learning material.

And as I've said, any time you spend researching the best materials to buy will have been better spent actually practicing the language.

I don't give the previous or following recommendations as examples of the one and only way to learn a language, but as guidelines you should consider that I have found work for many people. Even if there is theoretically a perfect course out there for you, it would be wiser to spend your time on an *okay* course and really make progress, than spend all your time and energy searching for that perfect course. Your energy should go into language learning, not course research. Buy an affordable course (or find a free online alternative, such as Duolingo), use it, and get active in other ways with your language learning!

What About My Learning Style?

The courses I recommend are very visual: you read the rules and sentences as the majority of your input. Audio CDs may be included, but these are accessories to the main book-based course. I have found this works for me, but there are major problems with a visual learning approach, especially for languages that use the same script as your mother tongue; you have that mother tongue bias on how the words "should" be pronounced.

This is why many people opt for an entirely audio-based learning approach. I find this way is more efficient for those with a conversational focus, but there is still a lack of good materials. For those learning (Mandarin) Chinese, for instance, I find that Chinesepod.com—which has podcasts for learning Mandarin— does this excellently in various language levels with entirely audio-based explanations. Similarly, Japanesepod101.com does the same for Japanese. Both of these are paid access podcasts.

Other audio-based courses include Pimsleur and Michel Thomas, both of which don't rely on visual cues at all and get you more focused on the sounds of the language, which has huge advantages for communication-focused learners. These may or may not be worth the investment, depending on the language version and your learning style.

Beyond audio, there are methods that involve leaving courses and teachers or tutors aside altogether and deconstructing natural speech or text yourself. This option is way too difficult for most people, including me. I do think we need some kind of learner-oriented guidance in language learning, up to the B1-B2 level.

The trick is that there is no perfect answer; it depends on style. If you think you can learn better through visual means, see the books I recommend, and if you appreciate audio learning more, use podcasts or audio-based courses or, ideally, focus on getting private spoken lessons or engaging in a free exchange, since that would be way more interactive and tailored to your specific needs.

Language Log

Apart from the course you use, you should definitely have a goal with your language learning project, as I discussed in detail in chapter 2.

With this in mind, go to fi3m.com/forum and announce your mission to the world there! You can also go to Wordpress.com and create your own free blog, then link to it in Facebook. Or you can just make brief updates on your progress within Facebook or on another social media site. Some people prefer to write about their progress, while others prefer to post video updates on YouTube, or audio updates on SoundCloud if they consider themselves to be more audiophiles with their languages.

Even if you are not public about it, document your experience in some way that helps you feel a sense of achievement. Even just writing or typing in a private diary can make a world of difference.

Language Social Networking

As well as the Fluent in 3 Months forum, which is one of the most encouraging and active language learning forums online for those with a spoken focus in language learning, you can try How-to-Learn-Any-Language.com for a more technical focus, or search for forums specific to the language you are learning.

Whatever you do, don't take on this language learning challenge alone! When you see others struggling at the same level as you, they can be comrades to relate to. Others ahead of you can give you the advice you need to solve a particular problem you may be having right now, and you can feel proud of your level by helping those a little behind you.

Engaging in forums, such as those mentioned previously, commenting on blogs, tweeting, joining Facebook groups, and generally discussing language learning in any online community can give you what you need and help you understand your current problems.

As well as this: never forget in-person meet-ups!

Conversational Connectors

Anthony Lauder, a Brit living in Prague who reads my blog, introduced me to a great way to learn essential vocabulary. *Conversational connectors* help your side of the conversation expand beyond single-word answers.

As you can imagine, if someone asks you a question, you may only be able to provide a single-word answer, which abruptly ends the flow of the conversation. I might ask you how old you are, and you could say "Thirty-one" or "Thirty-one. You?" Or I might ask "How are you?" and you could say "Well" and feel bad that you are providing such short answers.

Conversational connectors are words or set phrases you learn in advance to help a conversation flow much more smoothly. These not only add buffer to a conversation, so you are speaking more, but they also help the other person feel like he or she is not doing most of the talking.

The initial examples Anthony gave me that can be applied in a versatile manner were to answer the two questions "How is your food?" and "Where are you from?"

He suggested that we answer the first not with "Good," but with "Thanks for asking. To tell you the truth, I must say that the food is good. Let me ask you the same question: What do you think of your food?" And answer the second not with "England" but with "To tell you the truth, I'm from England. Thanks for asking. Let me ask you: Where are you from?"

As you can see, we are using the exact same connector phrases, which are not directly relevant to the current conversation but are very effective in keeping the conversation flowing and establishing intimacy.

There are quite a lot of different conversational connectors you can learn or come up with yourself to fill otherwise silent moments in a conversation or expand on very short answers. In English we have many "filler" words, like "you know," "well," "so," which don't actually add any information to a sentence, but they make the interchange sound more relaxed. I always try to learn these as soon as possible to help with my sentence flow.

Anthony came up with the examples below, and as such they are sometimes more relevant to him (for example, he refers to what his wife has said). You can easily imagine similar phrases yourself that will be useful in keeping your conversation flowing with more than single-word answers. I would recommend you take this list and add in one or two examples of your own that you might use in that situation. Then translate them to your target language and learn those words as early as you can, since this will enable you to keep conversations flowing, even as a beginner.

To help you, I've provided translations of these examples in more than two dozen languages at fi3m.com/connectors.

Apologizing

Don't be upset, but . . .

It was a slip of the tongue.

I said it by mistake.

I am sorry that . . .

(Dis)agreeing

One hundred percent.

Without question.

Exactly right.

Most certainly.

Without doubt.

In no way . . .

That isn't true at all.

That is an exaggeration.

I really can't believe that.

In principle that is true, but . . .

Admittedly that is true, but . . .

That's one way to say it.

Only up to a certain point.

Certainly. Why not?

I agree.

Closing

That is all there is to say.

That is all for now.

To sum up . . .

And there is the problem.

I hope it is only a matter of time.

That remains to be seen.

Filler

Understandably.

Frankly speaking . . .

Between you and me . . .

Anyway . . .

Well then . . .

Well, as a matter of fact . . .

How can I put it?

I must say that . . .

First . . .

Second . . .

I would like you to know that . . .

I am afraid that . . .

Now and then it seems to me that . . .

After all . . .

As far as I am concerned . . .

More and more . . .

Actually . . .

All joking aside . . .

Now seriously . . .

Elaborating

To be more precise . . .

And what's more . . .

Since I am already talking about it . . .

I would like to emphasize that . . .

Should I explain in greater detail?

Allow me to say it another way.

That is to say . . .

Nevertheless . . .

Even though . . .

That sounds like . . .

And that is why . . .

....

Opening

Thank you very much.

That is a good question.

That is such a difficult question.

Once upon a time, long ago . . .

....

Passing

Can you tell me please . . . ?

Would you be interested in us talking about something else?

And what do you think?

....

Qualifying

To tell you the truth . . .

I presume that . . .

I hope that . . .

In my opinion . . .

If that is true . . .

I don't know exactly.

I would like to think that . . .

The way I see it is that . . .

As you may know . . .

I don't have a big interest in that.

If I understand correctly . . .

As you already know . . .

That isn't such a big problem.

That is a matter of opinion.

As far as I know . . .

I have the impression that . . .

It is usually true that . . .

You never know, but . . .

I haven't thought about it before, but . . .

If I am not mistaken . . .

I am not certain whether . . .

Like every other man/woman . . .

I have my own opinion on it, but . . .

I am not an expert, but . . .

....

Quoting

She said something like . . .

My wife/husband pointed out that . . .

Recently, I heard that . . .

My better half said . . .

....

Switching

Now it occurs to me that . . .

By the way . . .

I have an interesting story about it.

And besides that . . .

Oh, I nearly forgot . . .

And one more thing . . .

On the other hand . . .

Bilingual Dictionaries

There are countless free online or app-based dictionaries you can get access to. The following are some that I have found useful:

Wordreference.com: The most versatile in terms of number of languages. The dictionary itself can be very useful, but I also find the forum that discusses particular words and expressions to be helpful when something doesn't come up in the dictionary itself.

Wikipedia: A surprisingly great option on Wikipedia is to look up particular place names, technical accessories, and many common items in the language of interest and then see the list of translations available in the left-hand bar of the main article's page. The translated article *title* is enough to give you a good translation. This is especially useful when a single word can mean multiple things.

Google Translate or **Bing Translator:** You should never rely on automatic translations for most of your work, but they are good for getting the gist. I generally have Google Translate open while I'm having a live Skype session or use it to help me understand long texts I may find online.

Book-based dictionaries: When I start to learn a language, I find that the dictionary at the end of my phrase book (Lonely Planet, Berlitz, Assimil, Collins, etc.) tends to include the most essential vocabulary and be small enough to take with me in my pocket (although apps on my smartphone are obviously more versatile). Book dictionaries are harder to keep updated and may miss lots of important words unless they are very large and bulky, so I would recommend using digital alternatives beyond pocket dictionaries.

Monolingual dictionaries: The previous options are mostly for bilingual dictionaries. That is to say, you look up the word to find its translation, whether that is to or from your native language. When reading or hearing words, though, once you pass a certain level (usually for me, it's from B1 and up), you should opt to use monolingual dictionaries: Spanish–Spanish or French–French, etc. This will greatly facilitate the process through which you attempt to think through that language and not through translations the entire time.

Image searching: When you use your favorite search engine, you can set it to search for images rather than web pages. For beginners, this can be a great way to understand the meaning of a word without going through your native language, and you get used to not thinking via translations. In this case, use the search engine in that language. For instance, go to Google.fr for the French version of Google, Google.es for the Spanish one, etc., and click to image-search in that language.

Particular language dictionaries: The extent of free online or app-based dictionaries that are better for particular languages is too long to include here and may change with time, so check out fi3m.com/dict to see a list of the best dictionaries per language, both for bilingual and monolingual options.

Many More Resources

> "The difference between a stumbling block and
> a stepping stone is how high you raise your foot."
>
> —BENNY LEWIS

Don't let choosing which book or course to use be a stumbling block that slows you down for any reason. It should simply be a stepping stone that is part of your greater language learning journey, most of which involves practice, studying from other sources, and, hopefully, making good friends for life.

While many people think that the course or tool you buy is what decides your success in language learning, I hope I've shown you in this book that the greatest tool of all is your persistence and willingness to use the language with real people—or at least with real native books or native audiovisual media.

Even though a perfect language learning tool doesn't exist, you can definitely get further with good tools. The ones I've listed in this chapter are only some examples, but new ones crop up all the time, especially in the digital age where online cheap or free options are becoming more and more plentiful.

As such, I'll keep an up-to-date list of my favorite ways to help you learn languages more efficiently, as well as more thoughts that expand on concepts introduced in this chapter, and reviews of the best known language products, at fi3m.com/ch-10.

Conclusion

Language learning has truly changed my life, and it opened up doors for me in ways I cannot even begin to describe.

Because of this, it makes me so happy to see the many regular e-mails and comments I get from around the world on my blog and videos, telling me that someone has been inspired to learn a language when they didn't believe they could before. I feel so proud to have been a small part of their story in learning an entirely new means of communication with a different culture.

If you are curious about my travels and my story and background, or how I'm doing or where I am right now, feel free to read more about me on fi3m.com/benny.

You can also find me on my blog at Fluentin3Months.com, which has tons of articles related to language learning, and posting on Twitter (@irishpolyglot), Facebook.com/fluentin 3months, google.com/+bennylewis, youtube.com/irishpolyglot, and youtube.com/fluentinthreemonths. I really look forward to connecting with you and hearing your story and progress!

To help you go further with your language learning journey, you can find additions to this book, including interviews with many people mentioned throughout the pages, and much more in-depth explanations of the topics introduced at the chapter-specific links provided and at fi3m.com/book-plus.

If any of these words have helped you or inspired you to learn a language, please share your story with me! But most important of all, share your newfound encouragement and enthusiasm with other potential language learners so we can help bridge the gaps between cultures and remove barriers by learning one another's languages.

Even if you didn't learn a foreign language growing up, I hope I've convinced you that it's never too late to start this exciting journey. Thanks for reading, and don't forget to check out the many up-to-date additions to this book online. Best of luck on your language learning journey—make sure to start using your target language today!

> "The best time to plant a tree is twenty years ago.
> The second best time is now."

ABOUT THE AUTHOR

Benny Lewis would not describe himself as a linguist—in fact, he was distinctly mediocre at languages at school. But now, ten years on, he has learned to speak over a dozen languages, has travelled the world, and has countless friends in many different countries. How? His success is due to a change in mindset and approach—a process he has shared successfully with thousands who have discovered how to start speaking from day one. Benny's goal is to impart his insights so that everyone can see how knowing other languages can change your life.

To find out more about Benny Lewis, go to www.fluentin3months .com, subscribe to his YouTube channel, follow him on Twitter @irishpolyglot, or find him on Facebook.